**SunRise Academy**
1130 6th Street, NW
Washington, DC   20001

# FEARON'S

# Practical English

## SECOND EDITION

# FEARON'S
# Practical English
## SECOND EDITION

Marna Owen

**GLOBE FEARON**
EDUCATIONAL PUBLISHER
PARAMUS, NEW JERSEY

*Paramount Publishing*

**Pacemaker Curriculum Advisor: Stephen C. Larsen**

Stephen C. Larsen holds a B.S. and an M.S. in Speech Pathology from the University of Nebraska at Omaha, and an Ed.D. in Learning Disabilities from the University of Kansas. In the course of his career, Dr. Larsen has worked in the Teacher Corps on a Nebraska Indian Reservation, as a Fulbright senior lecturer in Portugal and Spain, and as a speech pathologist in the public schools. A full professor at the University of Texas at Austin, he has more than twenty years' experience as a teacher trainer on the university level. He is the author of sixty journal articles, three textbooks, and six widely used standardized tests including the Test of Written Learning (TOWL) and the Test of Adolescent Language (TOAL).

**Subject Area Consultants: M.B. Clarke and A.G. Clarke**

Both M.B. Clarke and A.G. Clarke earned Ph.D.s in English at the University of California, Berkeley. Together they have developed composition and reading materials for a wide range of educational publishers. Both also score national writing tests for the Educational Testing Service. M.B. Clarke teaches composition at the University of California, Davis, and A.G. Clarke teaches writing at American River College near Sacramento.

**Editors:** Emily Hutchinson and Karen Bernhaut
**Editorial Assistant:** Stacey Dozier
**Text Designer:** Dianne Platner
**Art Director:** Nancy Sharkey
**Production Manager:** Penny Gibson
**Production Editors:** Mary Dickinson and Nicole Cypher
**Desktop Specialist:** Eric Dawson
**Manufacturing Supervisor:** Della Smith
**Typography and Computer Graphics:** Teresa A. Holden
**Graphics Coordinator:** Joe C. Shines
**Illustrator:** John T. Smith
**Cover Design:** Mark Ong, Side by Side Studios
**Cover Photo:** Carol Havens/AllStock

**About the Cover Photograph:** *Carol Havens/AllStock.* In our increasingly complex society, the ability to read, write, and speak clearly is crucial in many everyday situations. A traveler unable to understand this maze of signs, for instance, could easily get lost in the wilderness. To find out how to use road signs and other transportation aids to get around, see Chapter 14.

**Other photos:** Hazel Hankin/Stock Boston 244, John Herr 2, 30, 82, 96, 108, 118, 130, 150, 176, 192, 220, 232, 282; Ron DiDonato 16; Laimute E. Druskis/Jeroboam, Inc. 46; Thomas D. Boyd 58; Michael Falconer 68; Richard Wheeler 138; Robert A. Isaacs Photography 204.

Printed in the United States of America      6 7 8 9 10 99

ISBN 835-91040-7

**GLOBE FEARON**
EDUCATIONAL PUBLISHER
PARAMUS, NEW JERSEY

*Paramount Publishing*

## A Note to the Student

Practical English skills are the useful kind of skills that help you get along in your daily life.

Can you quickly find any book you want in the library? Have you ever worried about taking an essay test or writing a book report? Do you understand all the information on your paycheck stub? Can you read a street map? Give someone good directions? Decide which item to buy by comparing labels or guarantees? Understand simple tax forms?

These are just a few of the practical English topics covered in this book. Some of the skills you will learn, like job interviewing and communicating at work, could help you earn more money. Others, like writing personal messages and using criticism, may improve your social life. And some skills, like finding good health care and following safety rules, could even save your life.

The purpose of this book is to make it easier for you to succeed at school, at work, and in the outside world. Chapter by chapter, you will strengthen your speaking, listening, reading, and writing skills. When you finish this book, you will know where to find the information you need. And you will be able to interpret that information once you find it. You will be more knowledgeable about common forms and documents. You will be a better problem-solver.

All through the book you'll find notes in the margins of the pages. These friendly notes are there to make you stop and think. Sometimes they comment on the material you're learning. Sometimes they give examples, and sometimes they remind you of something you already know.

Watch for the study aids throughout the book. At the beginning of every chapter, you'll find **learning objectives**. These will help you focus on the important points covered in the chapter. And you'll find **Words to Know**, a look ahead at the vocabulary you may find difficult. At the end of each chapter, a **summary** will give you a quick review of what you've just learned.

Everyone who put this book together worked hard to make it useful, interesting, and enjoyable. The rest is up to you. We wish you well in your studies. Our success is in your accomplishment.

# Unit One

# English for Learning

*Taking good notes is one of the best ways to remember new information. No one can remember everything the first time around.*

## Chapter Learning Objectives

- ☐ Identify three ways that study skills can be useful in everyday life.
- ☐ Take complete notes on who, what, where, when, and why something happened.
- ☐ Organize and interpret directions.
- ☐ Name three techniques for reviewing and remembering information in notes.

## Words to Know

**key words**   the most important written or spoken words in a sentence, paragraph, or text

**main idea**   the central thought or idea of information that is written or spoken

**organizing**   putting things into clear order

You read in the newspaper about a great clothing sale. You repeat the address of the store to yourself. Then you hop in the car and start driving. But halfway across town you can't remember the street number. You would ask someone for directions, but you're not really sure of the store's name. "I should have made a note," you say to yourself. "It would have helped me to remember."

## How English Skills Can Help

It's a fact. To get along in this world, you need to learn and remember new information almost daily. Sometimes what you need to learn and remember is as simple as finding a new clothing store. Or you may need to learn how to operate a VCR or read a bus schedule. Other everyday learning takes place in school.

## Brush Up on the Basics

*A paragraph has a topic sentence, at least three supporting sentences, and a concluding sentence.*

*Do you remember what a sentence is? If you need help, see Grammar 1 in the Reference Guide at the back of this book.*

Learning and remembering information is also important to your future. The world is constantly changing. Today, robots build cars, and computers give out money at the bank. Telephone answering machines talk to you and take your messages. Who will get the best jobs of the future? People who are best at adjusting to the changes in a fast-changing world.

Learning and practicing two English skills can help you. These skills are:

☐   Taking notes
☐   Following directions

## Practice

Use a separate piece of paper to answer these questions.

*Everyday English*

*When was the last time you read a sign on the street to help you get somewhere? What English skills were you using?*

1. Write down three everyday situations in which you read or listen to new information.

2. How can remembering information help you reach your goals? Write a paragraph to give examples.

3. Why is it a good idea to have a study partner while you are learning to take notes?

## Practical English Skill 1: Taking Notes

Taking notes is a helpful skill. The most common place you take notes is in the classroom. A history teacher may talk to you for 30 minutes about World War II. Or you may take a computer class. In either case, you write down the most important information in your notes and study it later.

You can also take notes outside the classroom. Imagine yourself watching a cooking show on TV. You could take notes to remember a step-by-step recipe. Or you could take notes on how to get to a new friend's house. There are a million and one uses for notes.

**English Tip**
*Before taking notes on anything, ask yourself this question: What bits of information are most important to remember?*

### How to Take Notes

You can take notes whether you are reading or listening. Taking notes involves writing down the fewest **key words** to get the most meaning. What key words should you look or listen for? Usually these words answer one or all of these questions:

☐ who

☐ what

☐ why

☐ how

☐ when

Answering these questions will help you remember the **main idea** of what you have heard or read. These questions will also help you remember important details and facts.

Here are two examples of information that you might hear or read. Following each example are notes. Read through them.

**Example 1: A history lesson from a book**

During World War II, the United States and its allies had to send secret messages back and forth. They wanted a code that the enemy could not read but that could be quickly decoded. They used many different codes. Some of them were mathematical codes. Some of them used nonsense words. One code even used a Native American language. Anyone who did not know the language found the message almost impossible to understand.

**Example 1: Notes**
WW II: U.S. and allies need codes. Some codes: math, nonsense, Native American language

**Example 2: Spoken directions to a friend's house**

Do you remember Anthony Jones? You know, the guy who always wears those weird hats. Remember, he's got a dog? Well, the meeting's at his house today at 1:30. Just go from your house to Main Street. Hey, did you know they are tearing down the old school on Main? Anyway, go north on

Main to Oak and turn right. Go about four blocks, or maybe it's five, I can never remember. I've got such a bad memory. His house is at 401 Oak. It's on the right. There's a big old green car sitting in the front. He's had that thing for a year and it still doesn't run.

---

**Example 2: Notes**
Meeting at Anthony's. 1:30 today. North on Main. Right on Oak. 401 on right. Green car in front.

---

## Practice

**Notes That Work for You**
*Write your notes in any form that works for you. Shorten or abbreviate words. Use short or long sentences, or don't use sentences at all. Just be sure to include the key words and the main idea.*

Use a separate piece of paper to answer these questions.

1. For each example, write the **who, what, where, when,** and **how** questions that were answered in the notes.

2. Did you get the main idea from the notes? If not, how would you change the notes?

### After You Take Notes

Notes are helpful only if you use them. If you are taking notes in class, review them the same day. Read them aloud to keep the information fresh. Talk them over with a study partner. Or rewrite the information in a short paragraph. You may find something missing, or you may think of questions

**Everyday English**
*Look back at Example 2 on page 7. Is there something else you might ask your friend to help you find Anthony's house? When would be the best time to review your notes?*

that you want to have answered. For instance, in Example 1 on page 6, you might ask: What Native American language was it? Is the code still used today? Asking such questions helps you remember old information. And it also helps you learn new things along the way.

### Tips for Taking Notes

Here are the most important things to remember about taking notes:

1. Always keep paper and a pen or pencil handy.
2. Before you take notes, think about what you want to learn and how you will use the information.
3. Listen or read for key words. These words should answer the questions who, what, why, when, and how. They should also give you the main idea of what you are reading.
4. Notes should be short. They should have the fewest possible words and a lot of meaning.
5. Do not worry about writing complete sentences or using punctuation correctly.
6. Review your notes as needed—once a day for school notes is a good idea.

---

### Practice

**Everyday English**
*Where are good places to keep paper and a pen or pencil handy?*

Listen to the evening news for at least ten minutes. Take notes on three news stories. Follow the Tips for Taking Notes listed above. Bring your notes with you to class tomorrow. Be prepared to use your notes to report on what you learned.

## Practical English Skill 2: Following Directions

☐ You get ink on your new shirt. How do you get it clean?

☐ You have a homework assignment. How do you get started?

☐ You buy a package of noodles. How do you know how long to cook it?

Luckily, many of these everyday problems can be solved by following directions. Directions are everywhere. They are on the tags of your clothes and in your car manual. One-word directions (sometimes in the form of pictures) can be found on your telephone, TV, and VCR. Many of these directions are so easy to follow that you hardly ever think about them.

But what happens when directions are poorly written or hard to follow? Your first step is to **organize** the information.

*Everyday English*
*Is this sign a direction?*
*What does it tell you?*

## Organizing Information

Good step-by-step directions are written in the order in which they should be carried out. Recipes are often written this way. Here is an example:

1. Place about 1 inch of water in a pot and bring to a boil.
2. Add 4 cups of turnip greens.
3. Cover pot, and reduce flame to medium-low.
4. Simmer for 2–3 minutes, until greens are tender but still bright green.
5. Remove, drain, and place in a serving bowl.

You can see that these directions are clear and easy to follow.

But what if your teacher gives you these directions in class:

OK, I want everybody to finish this homework by Friday. I want a book report on *The Outsiders*. Turn in an outline by Wednesday because I want to make sure you're on the right track. Don't try to write the report without reading the book. Make the report three pages long and use your English book for help. Read Chapter 7 in your English book before you get started. It's on writing outlines and reports.

To turn these into good directions, you need to figure out the corrrect order of the steps. Here's how they might look:

1. Read Chapter 7.
2. Read the *The Outsiders*.
3. Do outline Tuesday and turn in Wednesday.

**English Makes Sense**
*Why do you think Step 1 is "Read Chapter 7," instead of "Read The Outsiders"?*

4. Get teacher's OK to do report.

5. Do report by Thursday. Three pages long.

6. Turn in report on Friday.

The directions are now step-by-step in the order in which they should be done. They are written in simple form. Sometimes, people in a hurry don't want to take the time to organize directions. But organizing can save you time and energy in the long run.

### Reading Directions Carefully

Once you have organized directions, you must read them carefully. This means reading each sentence slowly and out loud if necessary. Read sentences over and over again until you are sure you understand their meaning. Otherwise, costly mistakes can be made. Imagine what would happen if you baked a cake at 550° instead of 350°. What would happen if you connected the jumper cables on a car the wrong way? Problems like these can be avoided if you read directions thoroughly and carefully.

### Practice

Think of one situation in which misreading directions could be harmful. Write it down on a separate piece of paper. Then explain how you can keep such a disaster from happening to you.

## Tips for Following Directions

Here are some more helpful tips for following directions:

1. When you are listening to directions, take notes. Organize the information later if you need to.

2. Read through written directions before you do anything. Then you will know whether the information needs to be reorganized. A careful reading will tell you what you need and what is expected of you.

3. Have all the needed materials on hand before you carry out any steps. This will keep you focused and organized.

4. Read each step at least twice before you carry it out. Reading out loud sometimes gives you a clearer understanding.

5. Double-check what you've done after each step.

6. If you need help, ask for it. Product manuals often have toll-free numbers. Call this number if you don't understand something. Sometimes a friend or relative can help, too.

**Everyday English**

*What is something you learned how to do by following written or spoken directions?*

### Practice

Read the following directions. On a separate piece of paper, rewrite them in the order in which they should be done. Then do the steps.

Write your name (last name first) in the top right corner of a piece of paper. Write your teacher's name in the top left corner and the name of your school above that. Write down three things you learned to do by reading directions. Before you do any of this, make sure you look over the Tips for Following Directions on page 12.

# Chapter Review

## Chapter Summary

☐ Every day, for school, home, work, and play, you need to learn and remember information. Taking notes and following instructions are two skills that can make learning and remembering easier.

☐ Taking notes is a way to break down a lot of information into small pieces. Notes usually contain key words that help answer the questions **what, where, why, when,** and **how**. They help you remember the main idea of what a person said or wrote.

☐ Study notes for school are most useful if they are reviewed every day.

☐ Other notes, such as directions to a friend's house, should be reviewed just before you need to perform the task.

☐ Following directions is an important skill. Good directions are usually in step-by-step form. Sometimes you have to rewrite directions to get them in order. It is a good idea to read directions carefully before carrying them out.

## Putting Skills Together

Can note-taking and following directions work together? Think of at least one situation where the two go hand-in-hand. Write it down on a separate piece of paper.

## Developing Writing Skills

Patrick has just moved into his new place. Today is his first day in his new apartment. All at once he realizes all the things his mother used to do for him. Write a short story about Patrick and his first day on his own. Does he call his mother for advice? Does he read books on how to use the microwave oven? Include at least three situations in which he uses skills in note-taking and following directions.

## Chapter Quiz

Answer each of the following questions with two or three sentences. Use a separate piece of paper.

1. Why are note-taking and following directions called "everyday skills"?
2. What questions do good notes answer?
3. How detailed should notes be? Explain.
4. Should anyone be able to read your notes? Explain.
5. How can you make the most use of your school notes?
6. What are two tips for taking good notes?
7. What are two common situations in which you might need to follow directions?
8. You have a new cordless telephone. It comes with written directions on how to use it. What is the first thing you should do?
9. Why might you need to rewrite directions?
10. Why is it important to read directions carefully?

## Vocabulary Review

On a separate piece of paper, write the following sentences. Use the words in the box to fill in the blanks.

| key words | main idea | organizing |
|---|---|---|

1. The central thought in information that is written or spoken is called the _____ .
2. The most important words in written or spoken information are called the _____ .
3. Putting things into an order that is easily understood is called _____ .

## Chapter 2

# Using Books

*Using a dictionary is the best and quickest way to check usage and spelling. A dictionary is your most valuable reference book.*

## Chapter Learning Objectives

☐ Find information using the table of contents, index, appendix, and glossary.

☐ Scan headings for areas of interest.

☐ Interpret charts and graphs.

☐ Use illustrations to find information.

## Words to Know

**appendix**   additional information found in the back of a book

**caption**   words that tell about an illustration

**glossary**   at the back of a book, a list of definitions of special words in the book

**illustration**   drawing or photograph

**index**   at the back of a book, the list of subjects and the page numbers on which they can be found

**scan**   to look quickly through written material

**table of contents**   at the beginning of a book or magazine, the list of chapters or articles

**trend**   a general movement in a certain direction

You've finally saved enough money for that "new" used car. You know the make and color you want. But there are still a lot of things to learn. Which year and model have the best repair record? How safe is the car you want? What is a fair price to pay?

To find answers to these questions, you check out *How to Buy a Good Used Car* from the library. The book is more than 300 pages long. Do you have to read all 300 pages to find what you want to know?

Of course not. Good books and magazines have some "built-in features," just as cars do. These features can help you find information quickly and easily. All you need are the English skills to make them work for you.

## Practical English Skill 1: Interpret the Table of Contents

At the beginning of most books and magazines is the **table of contents**. The table of contents lists all the titles of chapters or articles and the pages on which they begin. Sometimes the table of contents gives a description of what is in each chapter or article. Look at this example of a table of contents.

### How to Buy a Good Used Car

### Table of Contents

| | | |
|---|---|---|
| Introduction | | 1 |
| Chapter 1: | Why Buy a Used Car? | 8 |
| Chapter 2: | How to Judge a Used Car | 24 |
| Chapter 3: | What's a Fair Price? | 36 |
| Chapter 4: | The Law and Used Cars | 42 |
| Chapter 5: | Which Car Is Right For You? | 56 |
| Chapter 6: | The Best Cars of 1970–1975 | 62 |
| Chapter 7: | The Best Cars of 1976–1980 | 150 |
| Chapter 8: | The Best Cars of 1981–1985 | 262 |

**Brush Up
on the Basics**

*A sentence has a subject and a predicate. A complete sentence makes sense on its own.*
  *For more information on sentences, see Grammar 1–9 in the Reference Guide at the back of this book.*

## Practice

Using the example, write the answers to the following questions. Use a separate piece of paper.

1. Suppose you are worried about getting cheated. You want to know what rights you have if you buy a bad used car. Which chapter should you read? What page number does it start on?

2. You're interested in a 1976 model. Which chapter will tell you what you want to know? What page number does it start on?

3. Write a sentence or two on what you might find in Chapter 1.

## Practical English Skill 2: Interpret the Index

Suppose you want to look up a very specific piece of information about a car. You don't have to read an entire chapter. You can use the **index** to help you find what you want to know.

**English Makes Sense**
*Think about the ways the table of contents and index help the reader. When do you use either of these reader aids?*

The index is a list found in the back of many books. It lists the key subjects of the book in alphabetical order. It also gives the page numbers on which the subject can be found. Below is an example from the index of *How to Buy a Good Used Car*.

### Index

**A**

air conditioning, 161

alternators, 5, 10

   in certain makes, 9

**B**

batteries, 21–55

   acid leaking from, 35

   used, 27

### Take a Closer Look

Notice that some of the subjects are broken down into subheadings. For example, you can find general information under the heading "batteries." The two subheadings under batteries tell you where to find specific information. For example, used batteries are discussed on page 27.

Indexes do not list every subject in the book. And sometimes the subjects you are looking for are not easy to find. Before using an index, think of several ways a subject could be listed. For example, suppose you want to read about the dangers of leaking battery acid. You could look under **Acid, Battery,** or **Repair.** You would probably find what you're looking for under one of those headings.

---

### Practice

Use a separate piece of paper to answer these questions.

1. Use the index of this book. On what page number(s) will you find information on libraries?

2. Suppose you want to look up the repair record of a 1977 Graceland Classic car. List three subject headings you could look under.

## Practical English Skill 3: Use the Appendix and the Glossary

You are reading through a book. You come across the words: *See Appendix.* An **appendix** is a section found at the end of a book. It includes extra, helpful information. Sometimes maps, charts, and illustrations are in the appendix.

**English Makes Sense**
*When might a glossary be better to use than a dictionary?*

The **glossary** is another helpful section at the end of some books. The glossary is like a dictionary. It lists key words found in the book. It also lists their meanings.

### Practice

Use a separate piece of paper to answer these questions.

1. Look at the end of this book. Is there an appendix?

2. Look up the term *card catalog* in the glossary of this book. What is it?

3. What kind of information might be found in the appendix of *How to Buy a Good Used Car*? Write at least one idea.

## Practical English Skill 4: Use Headings

*Everyday English*
*Look in two other books.*
*See how many "built-in*
*features" you can find.*

Most books have built-in signposts called subtitles, or headings. The phrase *Practical English 4: Use Headings* just above this paragraph is a heading. Well-written headings tell you what you are about to read. When you are looking for specific information, **scan** the headings in a chapter. Skip the headings that do not look useful to you.

Try it yourself. Which heading in this chapter would you look under if you wanted to read about glossaries?

## Practical English Skill 5: Read Charts and Graphs

You finally find what you are looking for in the used car book. The information you need is neatly put together in a chart. A chart is a listing of facts in table form. Reading charts is an important language skill. Information is presented in rows (going across) and columns (going up and down). The example below shows how you can use the rows and columns to find information you want.

Average Number of Major Repairs Needed in First Year

|  | 1975 | 1976 | 1977 |
|---|---|---|---|
| Classic | 3 | 3 | 5 |
| Gopher | 1 | 1 | 0 |
| Rough Rider | 0 | 0 | 2 |

☐ The chart title tells you that you can find each car's first year repair record.

☐ The columns tell you the year the car was made.

☐ The rows tell you the model of the car.

To find the repair record of a 1977 Gopher, follow these steps:

1. Find the column labeled 1977.

2. Find the row labeled "Gopher."

3. Run one finger down the column and one finger across the row until they meet.

4. The box tells you the 1977 Gopher needed no major repairs in its first year.

## Practice

Use the chart to answer these questions. Write your answers on a separate piece of paper.

1. How many times was the 1976 Classic in the shop?

2. Which car listed had the worst repair record?

3. Which was the best year for the Gopher?

### The Pie Chart

A pie chart is a special kind of chart. Its "slices" stand for different numbers. A pie chart is often used to show how something is divided. The sizes of the "pie" pieces tell you how the different numbers compare to one another.

***Everyday English***
*Make your own pie graph of a school day. Divide the pie into two pieces: the time you spend in class and the hours you have of free time.*

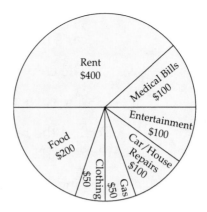

This pie chart shows one person's monthly budget. How much is in this person's budget for car repairs?

## Using Line Graphs

Imagine that you have just bought a 1982 Rough Rider. You have decided to take a road trip. You want to visit your cousin in Detroit, Michigan, in July. You need to figure out what kind of clothing you should take.

You go to the library and get *Michigan Travel Guide.* In the index, you look up "Detroit" and "temperatures." You turn to a page and find a line graph showing average monthly temperatures. Take a look at the line graph below.

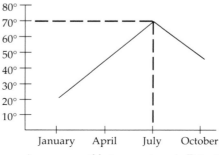

Average monthly temperatures in Detroit

The dotted line shows how you might find the average monthly temperature in July. Try it yourself, using these steps:

1. Put one finger on July.

2. Run your finger up the graph until it hits the point above July.

3. Now run your finger across the graph until you hit the temperatures.

4. You can see that it's around 70 degrees in July.

*What is a fashion trend? Can you think of an example?*

Line graphs also show **trends**. A trend is the general direction in which something is moving. The trend from January to July in Detroit is for temperatures to get warmer.

## Practice

Use the line graph to answer the following questions. Write your answers on a separate piece of paper.

1. What is the average monthly temperature in April?

2. What kind of clothing would you need to be comfortable in Detroit in January? Why?

3. What is Detroit's temperature trend from July to January?

## Using Bar Graphs

Books and magazines sometimes contain bar graphs. A bar graph uses bars or boxes to present information. Bar graphs can show trends and compare information.

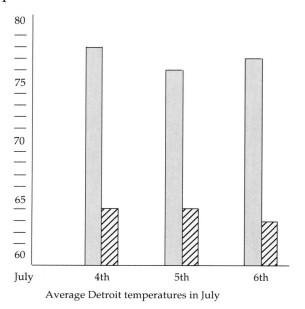

Average Detroit temperatures in July

This bar graph compares the high and low Detroit temperatures for three days in July. The solid bars show daytime high temperatures. The striped bars show nighttime low temperatures.

1. Put your finger on the striped box above July 4th.

2. Run your finger to the top of the box.

3. Run your finger directly across to the temperatures.

4. Your finger should show the temperature to be around 64 degrees.

You can also compare the daytime and nighttime temperatures for trends. Would you say it's warmer at night or in the daytime?

### Practice

1. What was the daytime temperature on July 4th?
2. What was the nighttime temperature on July 6th?
3. What might you pack to prepare for the difference in daytime and nighttime temperatures?

## Practical English Skill 6: Use Illustrations

You can get information by looking at **illustrations**. **Captions** (words that tell about the illustration) often add meaning to what you see. What do you learn from this illustration and its caption?

*Most auto mechanics learn their work on the job. Many also join apprenticeship programs. There they get classroom training as well.*

# Chapter Review

## Chapter Summary

☐ Books and magazines have built-in features. They are the table of contents, the index, the appendix, the glossary, and headings. These features are there to help you find information quickly and easily.

☐ Charts present information in a table form. A pie chart is a special kind of chart that divides information into pieces.

☐ Line graphs and bar graphs also present information. They are used for showing trends and comparing information.

☐ Illustrations and their captions can provide important information.

## Putting Skills Together

Which feature of a book or magazine could help you take notes? Give an example.

## Developing Writing Skills

Imagine that books no longer have the built-in features you read about in this chapter. Write a paragraph about how much harder it would be to find information in books. In your paragraph, discuss the table of contents, the index, the glossary, and headings.

## Chapter Quiz

Answer the following questions with one or two sentences.
Use a separate piece of paper.

1. What are four "built-in features" of most books?
2. How are these built-in features useful?
3. How are the index and the glossary alike and different from each other?
4. What is a pie chart?
5. What do the "slices" in a pie chart stand for?
6. When might you scan headings in a book?
7. What is a trend?
8. How is a bar graph different from a line graph?
9. How can illustrations be useful?
10. Explain why charts and graphs are useful.

## Vocabulary Review

Match each word on the left to its meaning on the right. Write
the numbers and corresponding letters on a separate piece of
paper.

1. index            a. list of words and their definitions
2. glossary         b. words that tell about an illustration
3. appendix         c. to look quickly through written material
4. scan             d. lists of subjects and the page numbers on which they can be found
5. caption          e. additional information in the back of a book

## Chapter 3

# Using the Library

*The card catalog at the library lists books by topic, author, and title. You can use it to find anything you need.*

## Chapter Learning Objectives

☐ List three reasons to use the library.

☐ Use the card catalog.

☐ Find books shelved by the Dewey Decimal System.

☐ Identify four types of reference books.

☐ Locate information in *The Reader's Guide to Periodical Literature.*

## Words to Know

**almanac**   book published each year that lists many facts, statistics, and other kinds of information

**atlas**   book that contains maps of cities, states, countries, and continents

**back issues**   previous, non-current issues of magazines or newspapers

**call number**   the Dewey Decimal number by which a nonfiction book is arranged on a library shelf

**card catalog**   file that contains list of books by title, subject, and author

**Dewey Decimal System**   system of numbering library books

**fiction**   literature such as novels and short stories

**literature**   writings in print

**nonfiction**   literature that is about true-to-life events or subjects

**periodicals**   magazines

**reference section**   section of the library containing the most-used books

Are you having problems making friends? Does your lower back ache? Do you want to escape to a South Seas island and forget about your troubles?

Believe it or not, the answers to all your problems may be at your local library. The library contains information on almost everything. You can find a book on how to be more popular. You can find a fitness magazine with advice on how to strengthen your back. And a good novel can take you to a land of coconuts and palm trees. With good English skills, you can use the library to help you with almost all your needs.

## Practical English Skill 1: Use the Library

Why should you bother using the library? Here are some of the library's most attractive features:

☐ There is no charge for borrowing library books.

☐ The library is set up to help you find what you need quickly and easily. And librarians are always on duty to help you with special requests.

☐ The library has books and magazines at different reading levels.

**English Makes Sense**
*Imagine your community without a library. How would people be affected? Name two ways.*

☐ The library is part of your community. Besides finding books and magazines in it, you can find out about many other community services. Information found in libraries can help you do your taxes. It can help you find a job. Some libraries even have programs to help improve your reading skills.

## Practice

Use a separate piece of paper to answer these questions.

1. Write at least three reasons for using the library.

2. Write about any visit you make to the library. What did you go there to find? How did you go about finding it?

## Practical English Skill 2: Use the Card Catalog

Imagine that you have gone to the library to find a book on job hunting. Also, a friend has asked you to pick up a book about her favorite sports star. She doesn't know the name of the book, but she does know who wrote it. The **card catalog** can help you find both the books you need.

**Everyday English**

Many libraries are putting their card catalogs on computer. They are keeping their old, "hard copy" catalogs, too. Which do you think would be easier to use? Tell why in two sentences.

The card catalog is a set of small file drawers with index cards in them. The index cards are in alphabetical order. You can look up books in three ways. The first way is by subject headings, such as "job-hunting," or "careers," or the type of job you want, such as "secretary." You can find books by the author's last name. And, finally, you can find books by looking under the title.

## Practice

Use a separate piece of paper to write the answers to these questions.

1. You want to find a book about collies, a special breed of dog. Name two subject headings you might look under in the card catalog.
2. You want to read a book by Bill Cosby. What would you look under in the card catalog?
3. Suppose you wrote a book called *All About Me*. What two headings would it be listed under in the card catalog?

### What's on the Card?

The cards in the card catalog tell you a little bit about each book. Take a look at the card below.

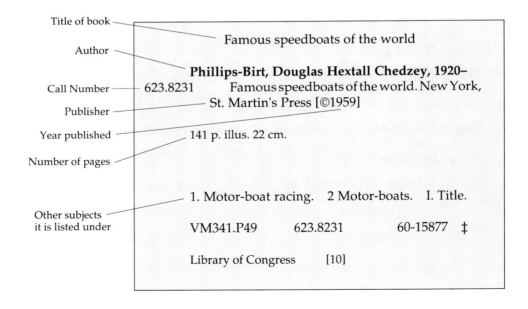

## Practice

Use the card to answer the following questions. Write your answers on a separate piece of paper.

1. What is the title of the book?
2. Who wrote it?
3. How many pages does it have?
4. Could you use this book to find information on a speedboat built in 1987? Explain your answer.
5. What other subjects could you look under in the card catalog to find books on the same subject?

## Practical English Skill 3: Locate Fiction and Nonfiction

The index card can also tell you if a book is **fiction** or **nonfiction**. Fiction is **literature** from the world of imagination. Nonfiction is about true-to-life events or subjects.

**Everyday English**
*Which do you like to read better, fiction or nonfiction? Would you choose a story about detectives, or an article on how to become a detective?*

To tell if a book is fiction or nonfiction, look at the top left side of the index card. If a book is fiction, you will see "F" or "Fiction" in place of the call number. To find fiction, you need to go to the Fiction section of the library. The books there are on the shelves in alphabetical order by the author's last names.

An index card for a nonfiction book will have a **call number.** This call number is part of the **Dewey Decimal System.** The Dewey Decimal System organizes books into different subject areas. For example, books about health care might begin with 616. Books about famous people's lives might begin with 200, and so on.

Nonfiction books are on the shelves in the order of their call numbers. A book with the call number 808.52 would be on the shelf before 808.53. A book with the call number 705.06 would be on the shelf before 705.14.

## Practice

On a separate piece of paper, put the following call numbers in order. Start with the lowest number.

| | | |
|---|---|---|
| 843.1 | 983.24 | 123.354 |
| 933.1 | 256.34 | 934.25 |
| 842 | 395.93 | 732.14 |

### The Reference Section

Sometimes, you will find "R", "Ref", or "Reference" in front of a call number. This tells you that the book you are looking for is in the reference section of the library.

The library's most-used books are in the reference section. Because they are so widely used, these books cannot be checked out. Four of the most important kinds of reference books are dictionaries, encyclopedias, almanacs, and atlases.

## Practical English Skill 4: Use the Dictionary

Dictionaries contain most of the words of the English language and their meanings. Large dictionaries also tell what part of speech each word is (noun, verb, and so on). They tell how each word is pronounced. Some give examples of how a word can be used. Some dictionaries even tell the origin of the word, or what language it came from. Besides looking up word meanings, the dictionary is a good place to check your spelling.

### Brush Up on the Basics

*Words are listed in alphabetical order in the dictionary. On a separate piece of paper, write the following words in alphabetical order.*

*sniff     smell*

*snake    sneeze*

*snarl     snag*

*shout     sneak*

*skeleton*

### Practice

> revise  (re-VĪZ)  *verb*
>
> to alter or change: I have *revised*  my opinion

Use this dictionary definition to answer the following questions. Write the answers on a separate piece of paper.

1. After something is revised, is it the same or different?
2. Does *revise* rhyme with *ice* or *eyes*?
3. Write a sentence using the word *revise*.

## Practical English Skill 5: Use Other Reference Books

### Encyclopedias

Suppose you need to do a report on the lost continent of Atlantis. The encyclopedia is a good place to start. An encyclopedia gives a summary of information on just about every subject you can think of. It is often made up of 10 or 20 books called *volumes*. Subjects are listed alphabetically in each volume. For instance, the subject heading *Atlantis* would be found in the volume labeled A.

**Library Manners**
*Some people take home books from the reference section. Other people keep library books way past their due date, or never return them at all. Why does this cause problems for other people?*

### Almanacs

**Almanacs** are mini-encyclopedias. They are full of facts. They tell a tiny bit about many subjects. Since most almanacs come out yearly, they contain the most current information. You could use an almanac to look up the date World War II started. You could use it to find out how much rain falls in Hawaii. You could even use it to find out who won the National Basketball Championship last year.

### Atlases

Are you going on a long road trip? Do you need to do a report on the country of India? An **atlas** can help you. Atlases contain maps of cities, states, countries, and continents. You might even find an atlas that contains maps of the moon!

## Practice

Which reference book would be best to help you find the following information? Choose from the words in the box. Write a sentence explaining each choice. Write your answers on a separate piece of paper.

| dictionary | encyclopedia | almanac | atlas |
|---|---|---|---|

1. You need to do a report on armadillos.
2. You are traveling across country. You want to see which cities you will be going through.
3. You and your friend are having an argument about which country won the most gold medals in the latest Olympics.
4. You want to know what it means to be "compliant."

## Practical English Skill 6: Find Articles in Magazines

You want to find out the latest news on sports cars. The encyclopedia does not have the most current information. The almanac tells you who won the Indianapolis 500 last year but nothing else. Can the library help you?

Yes. Libraries have the latest issues of many magazines, or **periodicals**. They also have many earlier **back issues** of periodicals. To find articles listed in these periodicals, you can use *The Reader's Guide to Periodical Literature.*

*The Reader's Guide* is found in the reference section of the library. *The Reader's Guide* is made up of many volumes. Each volume lists magazine articles published during a certain time. For example, the front of a *Reader's Guide* may say:

*Includes indexing from October 15 to November 4, 1988*

This tells you that articles published during that time are listed in that volume.

In the *Reader's Guide*, articles are grouped together by subject. The subjects are listed in alphabetical order. To find the latest articles on sports cars, you would

1. Find the *Reader's Guide* volume that lists the most recent articles.
2. Look up "Sports Cars."

This is what you would find:

**SPORTS CARS**

### Design

The affordable Porsche is axed . . . but new 944 looks smarter, goes faster. P.O. Bingham and T. Orme. il *Motor Trend* 40:21 O '88

Heavy breather! Corvette ZR1 [cover story] R. Grable. Morgan Plus Four turns sweet 16. M. Cotton. il *Motor Trend* 40:19 O '88

### History

25 years of greatness [Porsche 911] J. Karr. il *Motor Trend* 40:96-8+ O '88

Happy birthday, Corvette! [cover story] C. Gromer and B. Erdman. il *Popular Mechanics* 165:58-60+ S '88

### Testing

Chevrolet Corvette ZR1 [cover story] C. Csere. il *Car and Driver* 34:38-42 O '88

Ferrari F40 at Pista di Fiorano. D. Fuller. il *Motor Trend* 40:108-15 O '88

New toys for mom and dad [Buick Reatta, Ford Probe, Honda CRX, Mazda RX-7] D. Chaikin. il *Home Mechanix* 84:78-83+ O '88

That was then, this is now [Corvettes] R. Taylor. il *Popular Mechanics* 165:64-5+ S '88

## What the *Reader's Guide* Tells You

Look at the listings under Sports Cars. As you can see, the articles are broken down into three smaller groups: Design, History, and Testing.

The labels on this sample entry explain what information is given about each article.

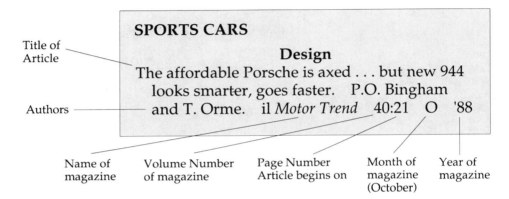

Title of Article

Authors

**SPORTS CARS**

**Design**

The affordable Porsche is axed . . . but new 944 looks smarter, goes faster.   P.O. Bingham and T. Orme.   il *Motor Trend*   40:21   O   '88

Name of magazine

Volume Number of magazine

Page Number Article begins on

Month of magazine (October)

Year of magazine

## Practice

Use the sample entry to answer the following questions. Write your answers on a separate piece of paper.

1. In which magazine will you find this article?

2. What page number does the article start on?

3. What do you think the article is about?

## The Friendly Librarian

Once you know which magazine you are looking for, how do you find it? Often, libraries post written instructions that tell you what to do. But if you are confused or need help, you can always ask a librarian.

Librarians can help you use the card catalog. They can help you think of subject names. They can help you find reference books. It is their job to help. Don't be afraid to ask for help if you need it.

### Tips on Using the Library

Most libraries are "user friendly." Use these tips to make the most of your library.

1. Libraries often have plenty of signs. They tell you how to use the card catalog, find magazines, or look up newspaper articles. Look for these signs and read them.

2. Ask your librarian for a tour. Get to know the library and its sections.

3. Remember that the library is a community resource. Read bulletin boards to find out about services and opportunities. And return books on time.

4. Always take a notebook and a pen or pencil to the library. Take notes to remember call numbers. Write down what you went there to find out!

**Library Manners**

*Suppose people never bothered to use the card catalog. Would that cause trouble for librarians? What would the library be like?*

# Chapter Review

## Chapter Summary

- ☐ The library is a place to find free information on many subjects. It is also a good place to find what is happening in the community.

- ☐ The card catalog is the library user's most important tool. It lists all books by title, subject, and author.

- ☐ Nonfiction books are organized with Dewey Decimal System call numbers. Fiction books are usually in a special fiction section. They are organized by the author's last name.

- ☐ The library's most-used books are in the reference section. They include dictionaries, encyclopedias, almanacs, and atlases.

- ☐ Magazine articles can be found by using *The Reader's Guide to Periodical Literature*.

- ☐ The librarian is an important library resource.

## Putting Skills Together

How might you use the index of an atlas? Write one example on a separate piece of paper.

## Developing Writing Skills

Imagine that the library in your city might be closed. The city does not have enough money, and cuts have to be made somewhere. Write a letter to the City Council. Give three reasons that you think the library should be kept open.

## Chapter Quiz

Use a separate piece of paper to answer these questions. Write one or two sentences for each answer.

1. What are three good reasons to use the library?
2. What are the two ways books are listed in the card catalog?
3. What is a call number?
4. How would you know that a book is fiction by looking at an index card?
5. How would you know that a book is in the reference section by looking at an index card?
6. Name two reasons to use a dictionary.
7. How is an almanac different from an encyclopedia?
8. When might you use an atlas?
9. What is *The Reader's Guide to Periodical Literature*?
10. Explain why you might use magazines instead of an encyclopedia.

## Vocabulary Review

On a separate piece of paper, write the following sentences. Use the words in the box to fill in the blanks.

| card catalog | call number | Dewey Decimal System |
|---|---|---|

1. Nonfiction books are numbered according to the _____.

2. All library books are listed by author and subject in the _____ .

3. The number by which a nonfiction book is filed on a library shelf is the _____ .

# Chapter *4* Passing Tests

*Taking tests is much easier if you plan ahead of time. It helps to go over your notes with a study partner.*

## Chapter Learning Objectives

☐ Identify three kinds of tests.

☐ List two skills for taking each kind of test.

☐ Name at least three resources that help a person to prepare for tests.

☐ Explain at least three study techniques.

☐ Identify four good study conditions.

## Words to Know

**analyze**   to figure something out; to interpret information

**essay test**   test that asks a person to write at least one paragraph on a certain subject

**objective test**   test that asks a person to choose one answer over another

**short-answer test**   test that asks a person to write one or two sentences to answer a question

**summarize**   to write or tell the major events or ideas without using details

A young man wakes up in a cold sweat. His stomach aches. His head hurts. Does he have the flu? No. He is thinking about tomorrow, when he must take two final exams. He is upset about taking tests.

*Everyday English*
*Think of one situation in the future in which you might need to take a test.*

Good test scores are often the way to a better job and a better education. You have probably taken hundreds of tests in school. In the future, you may take a high school competency test or an equivalency exam (GED). You may take a test to get a job or to get into college. Testing is a part of everyday life. Yet experts say that about 90% of people do not feel good about their test-taking skills. Good English skills can help you be more confident about taking tests. Doing well on tests is what this chapter is about.

## Practical English Skill 1: Identify Kinds of Tests

### What Kind of Test Is It?

Usually, you will know ahead of time the kind of test you are preparing for. Perhaps you will be asked to write about a subject. Or maybe you will be asked to follow written instructions while you perform a job-related task. Knowing what kind of test you are going to take will help you prepare for it. The most common kinds of tests are

☐ Objective tests

☐ Short answer tests

☐ Essay tests

You need certain skills to take each type of test.

### Objective Tests

**Objective tests** ask you to choose a right answer from one or more wrong answers. Some examples of objective tests are

☐ True/False

☐ Multiple Choice

☐ Fill in the Blank

The GED and many college entrance exams are objective tests. In the GED, you are given a problem or asked to read about a subject. Then you are asked to choose one of five answers given to you.

**Test-Taking Tips**

Here are some things to keep in mind when you take an objective test:

1. Answers that have "always" or "never" in them are usually false.

2. Read questions and answers carefully. A word such as *not, never, except,* and *always* is a key to a sentence's meaning. Missing such a word can cause you to choose a wrong answer.

3. The first answer you choose is usually the right answer. Unless you are absolutely sure you were wrong, stick with your first choice.

4. You may not be sure of an answer on a multiple-choice test right away. Begin by crossing off the answers that are clearly wrong. When you have narrowed your choices, take a guess. On most objective tests, it is better to answer a question than to leave it blank.

Here is an example of how a person might think while chosing an answer:

1. An objective test asks the test-taker to
   a. Give an opinion.
   b. Never guess at answers.
   c. Make choices.

*Everyday English*
*Are written tests the only way to find out about a person's knowledge or skills? What other ways might there be?*

### Practice

Choose the best answer to each of the following questions. Then explain why you did not choose the other two answers. (Use the example as a model.) Write your answers on a separate piece of paper.

1. Guessing at the answer on an objective test is
   a.  Always the right thing to do.
   b.  Never the right thing to do.
   c.  Usually better than not answering at all.
2. On an objective test, it is best to
   a.  Read for key words.
   b.  Never change the first answer you pick.
   c.  Write in ink.

## Practical English Skill 2: Take Short-Answer Tests

On some tests you will read these directions:

*Use no more than two or three sentences to answer each of the following questions.*

**Use Your Skills**
*What kind of tests are the chapter quizzes in this book?*

These directions let you know that you're about to take a **short-answer test**. The best answers on such a test contain only key information. Answers should be direct and to the point. They should not contain any information that was not asked for. And the answers must be written in complete sentences. Look at the following two examples. They give an idea of the correct way and the wrong way to write a short answer.

Question: How are short-answer tests different from objective tests?

**Example 1:**
Objective tests = make choices. Short answer = write full sentences. I like objective tests more.

**Example 2: Correct Way to Write a Short Answer**
In most objective tests, the test-taker must make a choice from a number of given answers. In short-answer tests, the test-taker must come up with the answer independently. Then the answer must be written in complete sentences.

---

### Practice

Explain why Example 1 is **not** the way to write a short answer. Give examples of what the person did wrong. Use a separate piece of paper.

## Practical English Skill 3: Take Essay Tests

**Brush Up on the Basics**

*Do you remember what a paragraph is? If you need help, look back at page 4 in Chapter 1.*

At some time you may be asked to take an **essay test**. Essay tests ask you to write at least one paragraph on a subject. What is the most important thing about taking an essay test? Know exactly what you are supposed to write about. Most often, you will be asked to either **summarize** or **analyze** a topic. There is a big difference between these two directions. To summarize a story or article, you would write about the major events or ideas. You would give only important facts. But if you are asked to analyze the article, you would go beyond the facts. You would give your opinion. You would interpret information and explain your thinking.

## Practice

Use a separate piece of paper to write answers to these questions.

1. Think about an argument that two of your friends or relatives had. In one paragraph, summarize the facts. Answer the who, what, why, where, when, and how questions. Be sure to write in complete sentences.

2. In the second paragraph, analyze the argument. Explain who you think was right, and why.

## Practical English Skill 4: Prepare for Tests

Imagine that you are preparing for a cross-country race. You get the advice of a coach and work up a training schedule. You run a certain number of miles every day. You clock your times. For support, you find other athletes to run with. You help each other train. By race day, you are feeling nervous but confident. You know you are prepared to do your best.

You can prepare for a test in the same way. To "train" for taking a test, begin by gathering resources. A resource is something you can use to help you. Here are some good "test-training" resources:

☐ **Test-Study books**   There are test-study books for the GED, SAT, government exams, and more. They contain sample tests and study skill practice. Use your library skills to find the books you need.

☐ **Classes**   There are many classes to help you prepare for the GED, and for high-school and college exams. These classes are often costly. But sometimes your school or a community college will offer these classes at a low price. Some classes are free, coming to you by TV!

☐ **Textbooks**   Usually, you will be studying from a textbook such as this one. Take notes and organize your material, using chapter headings.

☐ **The dictionary**   Keep this important reference book handy while you study.

☐ **A study partner**   You can help each other by discussing what you read and asking each other questions about it.

### Tips for Studying

How can you make the most of your study time? Here are some tips to help you.

1. Start studying well before test time. Do not wait until the last minute.

2. Studies show that people learn and remember more if they study for short periods each day. Try studying for one hour a day.

3. Study when you are fresh. Some people feel better in the early morning. Others feel good late at night.

4. Find a quiet place to study.

*Everyday English*
*What time of the day is best for you to study? Why?*

### Practice

Write down five examples of your own best study conditions. Think about the time of day and the clothing you wear.

# Chapter Review

## Chapter Summary

☐ Tests are part of everyday life. Passing tests is often a way to a better job or education.

☐ Three common kinds of tests are objective tests, short-answer tests, and essay tests. Each test requires a certain set of skills.

☐ There are many resources available to help you study for tests.

☐ Good study habits will help prepare you for tests.

## Putting Skills Together

What procedure should you follow when you are not sure of an answer on a multiple-choice test? Write the procedure in step-by-step order.

## Developing Writing Skills

Write an essay about your experience taking tests. Summarize the kinds of tests you have taken. Then analyze your feelings about taking tests.

## Chapter Quiz

Use a separate piece of paper to answer these questions. Write one or two sentences in each answer.

1. What are three situations that might require you to take a test?

2. What are three examples of objective tests?

3. How can reading carefully help you pass a multiple choice test?

4. Why are writing skills important for taking short-answer tests?

5. What is an essay test?

6. What is the difference between summarizing and analyzing information?

7. How can a library help you prepare for a test?

8. How can a study partner help you?

9. What are two good study habits?

10. How can taking good notes help you get ready for a test?

## Vocabulary Review

On a separate piece of paper, write the following sentences. Use the words in the box to fill in the blanks.

| essay test | summarize | objective test |
|---|---|---|

1. A test that asks you to write at least a paragraph is an

   _____ .

2. Multiple-choice tests are a kind of _____ .

3. To retell the main facts is a way to _____ .

# Unit Review

1. Write clear and simple directions telling someone how to get from your school to your house. Use enough detail so your visitor won't get lost.

2. Think about the last television show you watched. Answer the *what, where, why, when* and *how* questions about that show. Write at least five sentences.

3. Write three notes about the best piece of advice anyone ever gave you. Use key words in your sentences.

4. List two sections contained in the *appendix* of this book.

5. Explain the difference between the *Table of Contents* and the *Index*.

6. What part of this book is like a small dictionary.

7. Write a new caption for the photograph on the first page of Chapter Two in this book.

8. Explain why an *atlas* is not *fiction*.

9. What kind of publications are called *periodicals*?

10. In what section of the library would you find an *almanac*? Would *novels* be found in the same section? Why or why not?

11. Is it easier to *summarize* a topic or to *analyze* it? Explain your opinion in at least two sentences.

12. How is preparing for a test like preparing for an athletic contest? Name three ways.

# Unit Two

# English for Smart Shopping

## Chapter 5
English Skills and Advertising

## Chapter 6
English Skills for Buying

# English Skills and Advertising

*Advertising has a lot of influence on the decisions we make. Practical English skills help you make wise decisions.*

## Chapter Learning Objectives

☐ List three good reasons to analyze ads.

☐ Locate facts and opinions in ads.

☐ Identify misleading words in ads and explain how they are used.

☐ Use note-taking skills to make effective complaints.

## Words to Know

**ad copy**   spoken or written words in advertising

**comparative**   word used when saying how two things are alike or different

**consumer**   a person who buys goods and services

**emotions**   feelings

**evidence**   proof; statements that say something is true

**fact**   information that can be measured or proved as true

**opinion**   information based on a person's experience or thoughts; not a fact

You are driving down the street. Something catches your eye. It is a giant billboard. A healthy, smiling woman is holding cash. The words "Save Big at Jolly Stores" are at the bottom of the sign in big letters.

***English and Careers***
*Would English skills help you get a job in advertising? How? Explain.*

Believe it or not, some people are paid a lot of money to come up with words like those. Spoken or written words in advertising are called **ad copy**. Ad copy is aimed at getting you, the **consumer**, to buy something. By using some English skills, you can analyze any ad copy. Analyzing ad copy can help you to

☐ Know how truthful an ad is

☐ Decide how good a product or service is

☐ Save money

## Practical English Skill 1: Identify Facts and Opinions

**Everyday English**
Look at ads on buses or in magazines. Listen to ads on TV and radio. Does ad copy tend to be mostly fact or opinion? Why do you think this is true?

Ad copy usually contains two kinds of information. One kind is fact and the other is opinion.

A **fact** is a piece of information that can be measured or proved. Facts are usually proved with **evidence**, or more information to show that they are true. Think about the Jolly Stores' ad copy again: "Save Big at Jolly Stores." Is there any evidence to back up that statement? There *is* a woman holding up money. But is that enough?

The ad gives no real evidence that you will save money at Jolly Stores. At this point, the ad copy is only an **opinion**. An opinion is an idea that other people can agree or disagree with. Opinions often come from a person's own experience, values, or thoughts. It appears that the woman in the ad saved money at Jolly Stores. But there is no guarantee that you will.

When you read or listen to ads, analyze them for facts and opinions. Look for evidence. A list of low prices at Jolly stores would be better evidence than a woman holding money!

### Practice

**English and Advertising**
People who write ad copy often begin by filling out a fact sheet on a product. They include the most important facts in what they write.

Read and analyze the following ad copy. On a separate piece of paper, list the facts, evidence, and opinions in each ad. Then write whether you would be wise to buy the product based on the ad.

1. Use Nature Glo Shampoo. It leaves your hair healthy and alive! Its fresh smell will remind you of flowers.

2. Hamburger Heaven has the best-selling hamburgers in the state. We sell 17,000 burgers a day. You'll love them, too!

## Practical English Skill 2: Write Ad Copy

Think of a product that you like. On a separate piece of paper, list three facts and three opinions about the product. Then write ad copy for the product.

### Using Words to Suit Your Purpose

Suppose you are going to buy a new pair of jeans. One pair of jeans is advertised as "slim and slinky." The other set is advertised as "long-lasting." Based on those words, which would you be more likely to buy?

Words are powerful tools. Ad writers know that certain kinds of words will appeal to different kinds of people. The "slim and slinky" jeans will probably appeal to the **emotions**, or feelings, of young people. The "long-lasting" jeans will probably appeal to the emotions of people who are careful about money.

Unfortunately, words can be misleading. Watching out for misleading words can help you to analyze ads.

*It's a Fact*
*More than 100 billion dollars is spent each year in the United States on advertising.*

## Brush Up on the Basics

*Most misleading words are adjectives. An adjective describes a noun (person, place, or thing). What are the two adjectives in this sentence?*

These fresh juicy peaches will make your mouth water!

*If you need to review adjectives, see Grammar 34-38 in the Reference Guide at the back of this book.*

## Misleading Words

A shopper picks up a box of cereal. On the front, it says "Natural." That sounds healthy. But being a smart shopper, the man reads the box more closely. The cereal is natural. There are no added chemicals. But it hardly has any vitamins or nutrients in it. The word *natural* is misleading. When you see it, you think you are getting a healthy food.

When you read an ad, you should be careful of misleading words. Such words are usually used to describe the product or what it can do. *New, fresh, natural, healthy, slick, light,* and *improved* are examples of words that can be misleading. Look for evidence to back up the words. Only then should you take the ad seriously.

## Practice

Use a separate piece of paper to answer these questions. Write two or three sentences in each answer. Use a separate piece of paper.

1. A brand of milk is called "Always Fresh." Are these words misleading? Explain your answer.

2. An ad has a picture of a car. Under the picture are these words: *An amazing car for amazing people.* Which words in the ad appeal to the emotions? Explain how the words could be misleading.

## More Misleading Words

"Get your clothes *brighter* and *whiter*."

"X-300 engine . . . *more powerful*"

"*Prettier* eyes with  Black Lash Makeup"

**Everyday English**
*Do you believe everything you read or see in ads?*

Such ad copy is using a special type of word called a **comparative**. When you use a comparative to compare two things, you are looking at how they are alike or different. The people who wrote the ad copy above did not say what they were comparing. Are the clothes brighter and whiter than clothes washed in plain water? Is the X-300 engine more powerful than a turtle? Whenever you see a comparative, ask yourself, "What is being compared?" When you use a comparative, be sure to point out the two things you are comparing.

## Practice

Write your own ad copy using the comparatives below. Make sure you include the two things you are comparing. Use a separate piece of paper.

1. more exciting
2. funnier
3. better than

## Practical English Skill 3: Complain About Ads

Let's face it. Ads do not have to be 100% truthful. Ads can show cartoon characters selling toothpaste. Ads can show people flying in outer space. And sometimes ads tell lies. Perhaps they advertise a wrong price. Or maybe they show a product doing something it cannot do. As a consumer, you can complain about these ads. The state and federal governments have agencies to stop false advertising. You can find their numbers listed under CONSUMER PROTECTION in the white pages of the telephone book. You can also look under other government agency listings.

### Notes for Being Heard

Before you complain, make notes on what you are going to say. Your notes should provide the following information:

☐ Who you are

☐ What you are complaining about

☐ Where you saw the ad

☐ When you saw it

☐ Why you think it is false

☐ How you found out it was false

You can complain in person or by telephone. Or you can write a letter. When you complain in person, stay calm. State your case. Ask for action. If you do not get help, ask to speak to another person.

If you complain by letter, use the example on the next page as a model.

Your address ——————————————————— 111 A Street
                                    Hatter, North Carolina 55589
The date ——————————————————— September 1, 1995

The Department or
Agency you're ———————————— Consumer Complaints
writing to.                  False Advertising Division
                             Raleigh, North Carolina 55599

The greeting ——————————— Dear Consumer Complaints:

I am writing to complain about a false ad. The ad
appeared in the City News on August 1 of this year.
It stated that our local Jolly Store was having a
The body of the letter     storewide sale. When I went to Jolly Store, I found
explains why you are ————— only a few items on sale.
writing, what happened
and what you expect.

I believe this ad was false and should not be
allowed to run. Please let me know what you can
do about it.

The closing ——————————— Sincerely,

Your signature ———————— *Joe Jones*

Your name
typed or printed ————————— Joe Jones

---

## Practice

A newspaper ad said tapes were on sale at
Soundland for $4.99. When you got there, there
were no $4.99 tapes. The salesperson told you that
those tapes were poor quality anyway. He then
tried to sell you tapes for $8.99. The date was June
16th of this year.

Write a letter complaining about this false ad. Use
the model above.

# Chapter Review

---

## Chapter Summary

☐ Ads are designed to get you to buy. Analyzing ad copy can help you make smart buys.

☐ Begin to analyze ads by looking at facts and opinions. Facts should be backed up by evidence.

☐ Look for misleading words such as "new and improved." Again, look for evidence to back up these words.

☐ Ad copy often uses comparative words without really comparing two things. This can be misleading.

☐ Note-taking skills can help you make effective complaints about ads.

## Putting Skills Together

Suppose you want to learn more about advertising and laws. What three subject headings could you look under in the card catalog of your library?

## Developing Writing Skills

Every year, a consumer group gives out awards to advertisers. But the awards are not for quality. They are for the most misleading ads. Which ad on TV or on the radio do you think is the most misleading? Why? Write a paragraph that contains facts about the ad and that also gives your opinions about it.

## Chapter Quiz

Use a separate sheet of paper to answer these questions. Write one or two sentences in each answer.

1. What are three reasons to analyze ads?
2. What is the difference between a fact and an opinion?
3. Write an example of ad copy that contains one fact.
4. Write an example of ad copy that contains one opinion.
5. Why might the word "natural" be misleading?
6. What is a comparative?
7. A soap is advertised as having a "cleaner smell." Rewrite the ad copy so that you know what is being compared.
8. When is an ad false?
9. How would you find the agency to complain to about false advertising?
10. What English skill can help you make an effective complaint? Explain.

## Vocabulary Review

Match the words on the left to their meanings on the right. Write the numbers and corresponding letters on a separate piece of paper.

1. ad copy        a. a person who buys goods and services
2. consumer       b. information that can be proved as true
3. fact           c. word used to compare two things
4. opinion        d. words written or spoken in ads
5. comparative    e. information based on thoughts or experience

# English Skills for Buying

*Careful shoppers do more than compare prices. They read the labels to make sure they know what they're buying.*

## Chapter Learning Objectives

☐ Define the three steps used in making good buys.

☐ Use reading and library skills to build a "buyer's vocabulary."

☐ Make a question guide for getting information about products and services.

☐ List pros and cons to help make buying decisions.

## Words to Know

**cons**   reasons against

**estimate**   guess at what something will cost

**product**   something for sale that has been manufactured or grown

**pros**   reasons for

**reference**   a person who can say whether a product or service is good or poor

**service**   a skill that a person offers, such as washing a car

**service contract**   a written agreement to provide a service

**warranty**   guarantee on a product or service

Shelly is upset. Her car is in the shop. At first, the mechanic said it would cost $100 to fix it. Now she is being charged $600! But here is the worst part: Shelly signed a paper saying that the mechanic had the right to do whatever he thought was needed. He didn't have to ask her to OK the repairs. Now Shelly thinks he did work that wasn't necessary. But what can she do?

Have you ever been unhappy with anything you paid for? Then the English skills in this chapter are for you. By practicing these skills, you can save money. You can get **products** and **services** that match your needs. You can be happy with what you pay for. And that is really what being a smart buyer is all about.

**Brush Up on the Basics**

*Do you remember how to punctuate sentences? If you need help, see Punctuation 1 in the Reference Guide at the back of this book.*

## Practice

Write two or three sentences about something you paid for and were unhappy with. Include one lesson you learned from that experience.

### Three Steps to a Good Buy

To make a good buy, use these three steps:

**1. Gather information about what you want to buy.**

This can be as simple as reading labels. Or it can mean reading magazine articles, talking to people, and taking notes. Most of the time, you will gather information on two or more similar products or services so you can compare them.

**2. List pros and cons.**

List the **pros,** or reasons for, and **cons,** or reasons against, buying at least two products or services. This will help you compare them. You can look at the good and bad features of one thing. This way, you will know exactly what you would be paying for.

**3. Make a decision based on your values.**

*Everyday English*
*Do you think people often make bad buying decisions? Explain.*

Your values are the things that are important to you. Some people think that saving money is the most important thing. Others do not care how much they pay—as long as they are happy with the quality of the goods or services.

## Practical English Skill 1: Gather Key Information

Begin with finding key information. Key information is anything that will help you decide for or against making a purchase. Key information is found on labels and packages. It is found in product booklets. It can also be found in a **service contract** such as the paper Shelly signed.

Here are some examples of key information found on labels. Suppose you are concerned about your weight. You go into a store to buy bread. You look at the product information on two brands of bread. You read that one slice of Brand X bread contains 100 calories and 4 grams of fat. One slice of Brand Y contains 80 calories and 1 gram of fat. You now have key information to make your buying decision. You would probably buy Brand Y.

*Use Your Skills*

*Suppose you do not like the taste of Branch Y bread. Is it still worth buying? Explain.*

### Words for Buying

How much key information you gather depends on what you are buying. For clothing, food, and other small buys, you may want to read only package labels. For big purchases, you will want to read sales information. You will want to talk to people who know about what you are buying. And you will probably want to read articles in consumer books and magazines. To make sense of this information, you will have to build a "buyer's vocabulary." Here are some examples of words and phrases that might be useful.

**As Is:** This usually means there is something wrong with what you're thinking of buying. Perhaps a piece of clothing is stained or torn. Perhaps a piece of furniture is scratched. Look closely at items that are marked "As Is." They usually cannot be returned.

**Bait and Switch:** Stores sometimes advertise an item at a low price. But when the buyer asks for the item, the store does not have it. The salesperson will try to sell the buyer a more expensive item. This practice is called "bait and switch." It is illegal.

**Care manual:** Most products come with a care manual. This manual will help the buyer learn how to operate and take care of the item.

**Full Warranty:** A **warranty** is a guarantee that a product or service is good. Full warranties *usually* cover the cost of all parts and labor for a certain period of time.

**Labor:** Work done to repair an item.

**Limited Warranty:** A warranty that covers only some costs or kinds of repairs on an item. The buyer must read limited warranties carefully to know just what is covered.

**RDA:** This abbreviation stands for *recommended daily allowance*. RDA tells what percentage of recommended daily vitamins you're getting in a serving of food.

**Service Contract:** This is "repair" insurance for an item. For example, a buyer buys a stereo. The store offers to sell him a service contract for $100. The service contract states that for one year, the store will fix or replace the stereo at no cost to the customer. Buying a service contract is like buying a limited warranty. Read it carefully.

**Unit Pricing:** This method lets the buyer know exactly how much of a product he or she is getting for the money. Unit pricing is most often done with foods in grocery stores. Small labels on the shelves below products spell out the "price per unit." A unit may be an ounce, a pound, or any measure.

> Example: You see two boxes of cereal. Brand A costs $3.29 and weighs 24 ounces. Brand B costs $3.10 and weighs 16 ounces. Which box of cereal gives you the best value?
>
> Brand A Unit Price = 14 cents per ounce
>
> Brand B Unit Price = 19 cents per ounce
>
> Brand A is a better buy.

## Practice

1. A cereal box says that a one-ounce serving without milk has 25% of the RDA of Vitamin A. What does that mean?

2. A piece of clothing is labeled "As Is." What does that mean?

3. What kinds of key information should you look for in a limited warranty?

### Ways to Build a Buyer's Vocabulary

This chapter is too short to introduce every word a buyer should know. But your English skills from Unit 1 can help you build your own buyer's vocabulary. For example, a cereal box contains "riboflavin." What is riboflavin? Look it up in the dictionary. Do you want to know more about it? Look it up in the encyclopedia. Do you want to know more about nutrition in general? Look up

---

**Brush Up on the Basics**

*Do you remember where to find encyclopedias? Do you remember how to use them? If you need help, look back at Chapter 3, page 38.*

**Everyday English**
*What are some words in your buyer's vocabulary? List at least three.*

"Nutrition" in the card catalog. Soon a whole new vocabulary about health will be yours.

Sometimes, certain words will not be in a reference book. Suppose you want to know what "digital audio sound" is. You may need to read a current magazine article about stereos. Where will you find such an article? Look in the *Reader's Guide to Periodical Literature* under Stereos.

Gathering information does not stop at building vocabulary. Consumer books and magazines compare the features of hundreds of products. Look them up in your library. Then use the index, glossary, charts, and graphs to find what you need.

## Practice

Use a separate piece of paper to answer these questions. Write two or three sentences in each answer. Review the skills you learned in Unit 1 for ideas.

1. *Cholesterol* amount is sometimes listed on food labels. Sam wants to know what *cholesterol* is. What are two reference books he can use to find out?

**Everyday English**
*What key information can you find on clothing labels?*

2. Diane's doctor tells her that she is allergic to synthetic clothing. What reference book might give her a list of synthetic fabrics?

3. Todd's friend Bill says his new car must have fuel injection. Bill doesn't explain what fuel injection is. Todd gets a book on cars. In what part of the book should Todd look for a definition of *fuel injection*?

4. What part of the book would Todd use to see if there is a whole chapter on fuel injection?

### Make a Question Guide

Another useful way to gather information is to ask questions and take notes. Begin by making up a question guide. The question guide should contain the who, what, where, why, when, and how questions. Suppose you are looking for an auto body shop to repair your car. You will probably take the car into at least two shops for **estimates**. Your question guide will help you compare exactly what you will get for each price. Here is an example of a question guide:

1. What does the estimate include? If the actual work costs more, will I have to pay it?

2. Who else have you done work for? Can I get **references**?

3. When can you do the work?

4. How long will it take?

5. What kind of warranty do you give?

6. What if I am not satisfied? Will you charge me more for fixing what I do not like?

7. Where do you get your parts? Are they new or used?

---

### Practice

Imagine that you want to join a health club. Make a question guide for information you want to know. Write the questions on a separate piece of paper.

## Practical English Skill 2: List Pros and Cons

Once you have gathered your information, what do you do with it? Make a list, breaking the information into pros and cons. Such a list will help you compare two or more things easily.

Here are the pros and cons for joining two health clubs:

### Health Club One

| Pros | Cons |
|------|------|
| 1. New equipment | 1. No public parking |
| 2. Good trainers | 2. Short hours |
| 3. Nice locker room | 3. Crowded |
| 4. Close to my work | 4. No swimming pool |
| 5. Costs less than Health Club Two | |

### Health Club Two

| Pros | Cons |
|------|------|
| 1. New equipment | 1. Locker room has mold |
| 2. Good trainers | 2. Costs $100 more |
| 3. Swimming pool | 3. Crowded |
| 4. Free parking | |
| 5. Long hours | |

## Practice

Think of two restaurants you like. List at least two pros and cons for each.

## Practical English Skill 3: Look at Your Values

**Word Games**

*Another word for* pro *is* favorable. *What is another word for* con*?*

Once you have listed pros and cons, you must think about your values. Values are the things that are most important to you. Think back to the health club example. If saving money is very important to you, then you'll probably go with Health Club One. But what if you really enjoy swimming? Then you might pay the extra money for Health Club Two. Whatever your choice, you know that what you are getting is close to what you want. That is the key to being a good buyer.

## Practice

Use a separate piece of paper to answer these questions.

1. Look back at the pros and cons on page 76. Which health club would you choose and why?

2. Look at your pros and cons for restaurants. Imagine you have to choose the better restaurant. Which would you choose and why? What does that say about your values?

# Chapter Review

## Chapter Summary

- ☐ English skills can help you be a smart consumer.

- ☐ To get the best buy, gather information. List pros and cons. Then use your values to make a final decision.

- ☐ Gather key information. Use labels, books, and magazines. Reference books and the library can help you build a "buyer's vocabulary."

- ☐ A question guide of who, what, when, where, why, and how questions can be used to get key information. Take notes to compare what you find.

## Putting Skills Together

Suppose you are unhappy with a product or service. How could you use the library to find out who to complain to?

## Developing Writing Skills

Suppose you are unhappy with the service you were given in a hotel. The desk clerk was rude to you. The food was terrible. And you paid quite a bit. Write a letter to the hotel complaining about the service. Make sure you suggest how it could be improved.

## Use the Appendix

The Appendix of this book contains a Buyer's Vocabulary. Look up these words and write their meanings on a separate piece of paper.

1. unit pricing
2. labor

3. bait and switch
4. care manual

## Chapter Quiz

Use a separate piece of paper to answer these questions. Write one or two sentences in each answer.

1. What are three good reasons for being a smart buyer?

2. What are the three steps in smart buying?

3. Where will you find key information on food? On clothing? Give an example of each.

4. You are shopping for stereo speakers. The salesperson says Brand X speakers have the best woofers around. How can you find out what woofers are?

5. How can you find out more about Brand X's woofers compared to other brands?

6. What is a question guide, and how can it help you?

7. What are pros and cons?

## Vocabulary Review

Match the words on the left to their meanings on the right. Write the numbers and corresponding letters on a separate piece of paper.

1. warranty        a. reasons for

2. product         b. a person who can say whether a product or service is good or poor

3. service         c. guess at what something will cost

4. pros            d. guarantee

5. cons            e. something for sale

6. estimate        f. a skill that is offered

7. reference       g. reasons against

# Unit Review

1. What are messages from manufacturers to consumers called?

2. Think about an ad you often see on television. Use your own words to tell the main message of that ad.

3. Write two statements about a certain brand of bread. Use a *fact* in one statement and an *opinion* in the other.

4. Write ad copy for a new brand of paper towels. Use at least three words or phrases that will make your paper towels seem better than others.

5. Think of an ad you saw that was aimed at your *emotions*. Explain how that ad made you *feel* about the product.

6. Name two misleading words that are often used in advertising.

7. Explain the difference between a *warranty* and a *service contract*.

8. Name two ways to *gather information* about a product before you buy it.

9. Write three *pros* and *cons* about owning a large car. Then write two *pros* and *cons* about owning a small car.

10. Why is it important to get an *estimate* before leaving something at a repair shop? Explain in your own words.

11. How do your *values* affect the way you spend your money? Give an example from your own life.

# Unit Three

# English for Work

Chapter **7** Job-Hunting

*State employment offices post many different job listings.*
*Want ads and bulletin boards are other good sources.*

## Chapter Learning Objectives

- [ ] Develop an interview guide to learn about goals, interests, and jobs.
- [ ] Scan a bulletin board for job information.
- [ ] Identify three ways the phone book can help with job-hunting.
- [ ] Locate appropriate jobs in the want ads.
- [ ] Write and edit a "Work Wanted" ad.

## Words to Know

**edit**   to improve writing by making changes

**fee**   money charged for a service

**goals**   things a person wants to achieve

**interests**   concerns or hobbies

**network**   the people you contact to help you get
information about jobs

Kevin always wanted to be a waiter in a good restaurant. He saw himself charming the customers. He would earn big money in tips.

Kevin finally got a job as a waiter. But it was not as easy as he thought it was going to be. He was on his feet for six-hour shifts. He had to be polite to rude people. He had to carry heavy trays and make it look easy. By the end of his first week, Kevin was not sure that being a waiter was for him.

Not many people find dream jobs. But the practical English skills in this chapter can help you. By using these skills, you can find a job that comes close to fitting your needs.

## Practical English Skill 1: Develop an Interview Guide

Everyone has different goals and interests when it comes to work. A construction worker might have to do hard, dirty work. A strong person who likes to work outdoors may enjoy the job. A child-care worker may make only $5.00 per hour. But suppose that he loves working with children. The money is not the most important thing to him. The best jobs are the ones that match your goals and interests.

The first task in job-hunting is to get clear about your own **goals** and **interests.** Goals are things you want to achieve. If you want to make $50,000 per year, that is a goal. If you want to own a restaurant, that is a goal. Your interests are things that are important to you, or things that you are curious about. You may have interests in computers or in keeping parks clean. Knowing your own interests can lead you to meaningful work.

*Everyday English*

*How do you think reading and thinking skills can help you find a job?*

How do you discover your goals and interests? Interview yourself. Begin by using your English skills to write a self-interview guide. Interview guides begin with those familiar words: *who, what, where, why, when,* and *how.* Here is an example of one person's self-interview guide.

### Self-Interview Guide

1. What skills do I already have? What do I know how to do?

2. What are the things I most like to do?

3. What are skills I would like to learn?

4. Where would I like to work? In a building or outside? In what part of the city?

**Interest Tests**

*Some employers give interest tests. These tests have no right or wrong answers. They are designed to help you learn where your interests lie.*

5. When can I work? Do I need certain hours? Will a midnight shift do?

6. Why do I want a job? Am I willing to work for less money now, while I can learn skills that will help me later?

Once you answer these questions, begin to analyze yourself. Are you an outgoing, friendly person? Or are you better with machines? Do you like to work with your hands? Would you be happiest sitting at a desk or moving around? As you answer these questions, you will get to know yourself better. And you will have a better idea of what kind of job to look for.

## Practice

On a separate piece of paper, make up your own interview guide. Begin with questions from the example and add at least two questions of your own. Then answer the questions.

## Practical English Skill 2: Use Several Methods for Job-Hunting

Once you know your goals and interests, how do you find a job? There are many resources. There are employment agencies and want ads in newspapers. There are signs in windows and people with leads. And there are workers to give you information. A few practical English skills can help you use these resources effectively.

## Method 1: Networking

How do you form **networks** with people? Making a network means meeting people, learning about jobs, and getting leads. You begin to build a network by meeting people who have the kind of job you think you want. Then, you can use interview questions to learn more about the job. If you feel comfortable, ask the person for leads. Here is how Kevin interviewed a waiter one night when he was out to dinner.

Kevin: *So, how do you like being a waiter?*

Waiter: *It's OK. I make good tips.*

Kevin: *May I ask how much?*

Waiter: *Oh, maybe $30 per night, $50 on the weekends.*

Kevin: *What don't you like about your job?*

Waiter: *The hours. You make the best money working weekend nights. That doesn't leave much time for dating. And my feet hurt almost all the time. It's hard work.*

Kevin: *What kind of skills do waiters need?*

Waiter: *You need to be patient. Some customers can really be mean. You need to have good balance so you can carry trays. Of course, you've got to have a good memory. For taking orders, you know. Oh, and then you have to be able to add up bills. There's a lot to it.*

Kevin: *What are the chances of me getting a job here?*

Waiter: *I'll let you know when an opening comes up. Leave me your name and phone number.*

*Practice Your Skills*
*Does waiting tables fit in with your goals and interests? Explain.*

## Practice

What would it be like to be a teacher? Write an interview guide to find out. Use the who, what, where, when, and why words to help you. Ask your favorite teacher for an interview. Take notes on what you find. Does teaching fit your goals and interests?

## Method 2: Scan for Job Information

*Everyday English*
*Where are jobs posted in your area?*

Back in Chapter 2, you practiced scanning headings in books. You can also use your scanning skills to find jobs. You can scan store windows for "Help Wanted" and "Now Hiring" signs. You can read neighborhood bulletin boards for jobs.  When you see a bulletin board, quickly look over the notices. Look for the words: *job, worker, pay,* and *work.*  You will probably find some information on an available job.

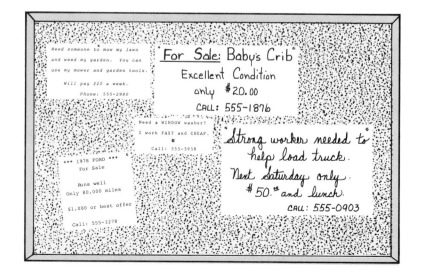

## Practice

Scan the bulletin board on page 87 for jobs. On a separate piece of paper, write the jobs that are available.

### Method 3: Use the Phone Book

One of the best resources a job-hunter has is the phone book. At the front of the white pages is a list of government agencies. They are usually divided into state, city, county, and federal listings. Under each section, you will usually find the heading "Employment" or "Economic Development." Agencies under these headings can help you get training and find jobs. There is usually no charge for using these agencies.

The yellow pages are also helpful for job-hunters. You can use the yellow pages to look up private employment agencies. These agencies can test your skills and find you work for a **fee**. You can also use the yellow pages to find a job in your field. Suppose you are looking for work as a pizza maker. You can look under the headings "Pizza" and "Restaurants." Then you can call the places listed to find out if they have any openings.

*Remember Your Library Skills*
*What section of the library do you think would contain phone books?*

## Practice

Use a separate piece of paper to answer these questions.

1. Jan wants to know if her city has employee training programs. Exactly how would she find out by using the telephone book?

2. Henry would like to find work as an airline flight attendant. What heading could he look under in the yellow pages to find out where to look?

3. What questions could Henry ask when he calls about the airline job? Develop an interview guide that he could use over the phone. Include at least five questions.

## Method 4: Read the Want Ads

One of the best places to look for a job is in the "Help Wanted" section of the newspaper. Help Wanted ads are in the "Classified" section.

To put want ads to work for you, follow these steps:

*Everyday English*
*Does it take the same skills to read the want ads as it does to read the card catalog?*

1. The job you want may be listed under several headings. For example, suppose you are looking for a job in sales. You could look under "Salesperson" or "Retail." Think of at least two possible headings before you start.

2. Scan the want ads for the job you want. The want ads are in alphabetical order.

3. Once you find an interesting ad, circle it.

4. Read the ad carefully. Find out what experience you need and how to apply.

## Practice

Do the following on a separate piece of paper.

1. Write the following jobs in alphabetical order: clerk, word processor, sales manager, cashier, accountant.

2. Suppose you are looking for a job as a grocery checkout person. What are two headings that you might look under in the want ads?

3. A want ad says: "Driver & odd jobs for florist. Must know Oakland streets, have neat appearance. 555-3333." What skills do you need for this job? How would you prepare for the interview? Write two or three sentences.

### Want Ad Abbreviations

Many times, want ads use abbreviations of words. Read this list of common abbreviations and their meanings.

| Abbreviation | Meaning |
| --- | --- |
| applic. | application (form you fill out when applying for a job) |
| exp. | experience |
| f/t. | full-time (40 hours per week) |
| p/t. | part-time (less than 40 hours per week) |
| nec. | necessary (something you must have) |
| pref. | preferred (what the employer would like you to have, though it is not necessary) |
| min. | minimum (the least amount) |

| | |
|---|---|
| refs. | references (people who can say what kind of person you are, how good a worker you are, and so on) |
| req. | required (something you must have) |
| temp. | temporary (job is for a limited period of time) |
| wk. | week |
| mos. | months |
| yrs. | years |

## Practice

On a separate piece of paper, write out the following want ad. Use the full word in place of the abbreviations.

Now hiring counter people p/t. and f/t. No exp. nec. Must be at least 16 yrs. old. Work min. of 10 hrs./wk. Pick up applic. at Freddy's, corner of Market and Main.

## Practical English Skill 3: Write and Edit "Work Wanted" Ads

Jenny didn't have to go out and look for a job. She placed an ad in the "Employment Wanted" section of her newspaper. She got several calls per day the first week.

"I like to hire people who advertise," said one employer. "I know they really want to work."

**Brush Up on the Basics**

*Do you remember how to punctuate abbreviations? If you need help, see Punctuation 2 in the Reference Guide at the back of this book.*

To write your own ad, you will need to include this information:

☐ The kind of job you want

☐ Your skills and experience

☐ Where you can be reached

☐ Whether you want part-time or full-time work

☐ Any other information you think is important

Ads usually cost you a certain amount of money per line. For that reason, it is a good idea to write two drafts of your want ad. In the first draft, write whatever you like. Include everything you think is important. Write in full sentences. In the second draft, cut out unnecessary words and information. Use abbreviations. This is called **editing** your work. Take a look at Jenny's first and second drafts for ideas.

**First Draft**

I am a college student looking for part-time work on nights and weekends. I have child-care skills and a driver's license, and I love children. I don't have a car, though. I have lots of references. Please call me at 555-1211 after 3 p.m. I would like to make $4.50 per hour.

**Edited Version**

Want p/t. child-care position on nights and wkends. Exp., license, refs. 555-1211 aft. 3 p.m. $4.50 per hour.

## Practice

On a separate piece of paper, edit the "work wanted" ad below. Keep it under 20 words. Abbreviations and phone numbers count as one word each.

*I am looking for work as a typist. I type 90 words per minute. I have worked at a number of offices and have lots of references. I am a good worker. Full-time work is preferred. Call Tom at 555-9990 just about anytime, except Saturdays and Sundays.*

# Chapter Review

## Chapter Summary

- [ ] Practical English skills can help you get a job that fits your interests and goals.

- [ ] Interview guides can help you learn about yourself and jobs. These guides are based on the *who, what, where, when, why,* and *how* questions.

- [ ] Scanning bulletin boards is a skill for quickly finding out about available jobs.

- [ ] The phone book can help you find government employment agencies. It can also help you find private employment agencies. Finally, you can use it to find jobs in a certain field.

- [ ] To read the want ads efficiently, know what you are looking for. Look for key information to help you prepare for a job interview.

- [ ] Work wanted ads can be a good way to find work. They should be brief and to the point. They should use abbreviations.

## Putting Skills Together

In Chapter 6, you listed pros and cons for buying products or services. How could you use pros and cons to help you choose a job? Give an example.

## Developing Writing Skills

Think about a job you would like to have. Write a "work wanted" ad. Write two drafts. In the first draft, use complete words and sentences. Edit the second draft so that it is under 17 words. Use abbreviations.

---

## Chapter Quiz

Use a separate piece of paper to answer these questions. Write one or two sentences in each answer.

1. What are two ways to use an interview guide?

2. Write two questions you would ask yourself to discover your interests and goals.

3. Write two examples of questions you would ask when you are building a network.

4. What key words would you scan bulletin boards for when you are looking for a job?

5. What headings would you look under to find government employment agencies?

6. How might you find private employment agencies in the yellow pages?

7. Brenda wants a job as a clothing salesperson. What two headings could she look under in the yellow pages to help her find clothing stores?

8. A want ad says "F/t. worker needed, temp. 4 wks. No exp. req., just refs." What does it mean?

9. Steve is a construction worker. He is skilled at putting on roofs. What two headings could he look under in the yellow pages to find work?

10. What are two reasons to use a "work wanted" ad?

## Vocabulary Review

On a separate piece of paper, write three sentences of your own. Use one or more of these "job-hunting" words in each sentence.

network                    fee                    goal

## Chapter 8

# Applying for Jobs

*Employers are impressed when job candidates fill out applications neatly and thoroughly. It's a good idea to proofread your application before you turn it in. Make sure you've filled in all the blanks.*

## Chapter Learning Objectives

☐ Write and edit a résumé.

☐ Identify three techniques for filling out applications.

☐ Write a cover letter.

## Words to Know

**accomplishments**   things done well

**action verbs**   words that show action like cook and clean

**application**   form employers ask job-seekers to fill out with information about themselves

**cover letter**   short letter to the employer included with job application or résumé

**duty**   task performed on a job

**proofread**   to carefully check writing for mistakes

**résumé**   written statement of a person's work experience, education, and personal information

**Career English**

*Some people would think the store owner acted unfairly. After all, she did not even look at the person's skills. What do you think?*

A store owner is looking over **résumés**. One résumé is a mess. It has words crossed out and smudges from an eraser. The store owner tosses it aside. "I wouldn't even think of hiring this person," she says to herself.

How can you keep your résumé or job **application** from landing in the wastebasket? You can begin by practicing the English skills in this chapter.

## Practical English Skill 1: Write a Résumé

A résumé is your written statement of your own background. It gives personal information, such as your address and phone number. It outlines your education and lists your work experience and skills.

To an employer, your résumé or job application is you. For that reason, your résumé must be neat and well-written. There are many different ways to put a résumé together. The example that follows shows the parts that all résumés should include.

|  | |
|---|---|
| Your name | **Thomas R. Brown** |
| Address | 1573 Jackson Street, Apartment 12 |
| | Sacramento, CA 95864 |
| Phone number | (408) 555-1263 |

The job you want.

**Objective:** Position as a salesperson in a computer retail store

Your schooling to date

**Education:** Graduated Monroe High School, 1990
Currently enrolled in Sacramento Community College, majoring in Computer Science

**Work Experience:**

6/94–6/95 Sandwich Maker. Sam's Sandwich Stand, 1484 Bridgeport Drive, Sacramento, CA 95825.

Made 100 sandwiches per eight-hour shift. Served customers, handled money. Ordered food supplies.

Paid or volunteer work experience. Include dates and duties.

5/93–5/94 Garden Helper. Mowed lawns, pruned trees, put in plants.

Any skills that might help you get the job.

**Skills:** Can operate personal computers and use 15 software packages.

People who will stand up for your character and work abilities.

**References:** Available upon request.

## Practice

On a separate piece of paper, write a first draft of your résumé. The first draft is just for getting information down on paper. Follow the model on page 98. If you do not have any paid work experience, think of work you have done at home or school. You may have skills in childcare, car repair, or yard work, for example.

## Practical English Skill 2: Use Action Verbs

**Brush Up on the Basics**

*Do you remember what a verb is? If you need help, see Grammar 17–19 in the Reference Guide at the back of this book.*

Once you have a first draft, you can edit your résumé. The most important part of your résumé tells about your work experience. Here, you want to use **action verbs** to describe your **duties** and skills. Action verbs are verbs that describe doing. *Run, jump,* and *crash* are action verbs. Action verbs give punch and color to your résumé. And they let you say a lot in a short space. Here are some examples of how Thomas Brown edited his résumé to include action verbs.

| **First draft** | **Second draft** |
|---|---|
| I <u>was</u> a sandwich maker. | <u>Made</u> sandwiches. |
| I <u>was</u> a waiter. | <u>Served</u> customers. |
| I also <u>had to take</u> money from customers. | <u>Handled</u> money. |
| Sometimes I <u>had to order</u> supplies. | <u>Ordered</u> supplies. |

*Everyday English*

*Can you think of a job where you wouldn't need a résumé or job application?*

## Practice

Edit these sentences. Make them short and to the point by using action verbs. Hint: Cut out verbs like *was, had, did, is,* and *were.* They do not show action. Find action verbs to replace them.

1. I was a babysitter for three children.
2. I did the ordering of food for the concession stands.
3. I had to call people on the phone about making their appointments.

## Practical English Skill 3: Edit Your Résumé

Can a résumé show how hard you work? Can it show how skilled you are? Thomas Brown tried to do this when he wrote "Made 100 sandwiches per eight-hour shift." This sentence helps employers know how much work Thomas can do in a day. It helps employers measure Thomas's skills.

When you edit your résumé, use numbers to help measure your skills. "Cared for children," "Cared for four children," and "Cared for 30 children," all give employers different pictures. You can also list any awards or honors. If you were top employee of the month, put it on your résumé. This is a way to show your **accomplishments**.

## Practice

Read the sentence pairs below. Choose the sentence that best measures a person's skills or duties. Write it on a separate piece of paper.

1. a. Answered phone.
   b. Answered six phone lines in office; averaged three calls per minute.
2. a. Was an excellent employee.
   b. Won "Employee of the Month" award four times in one year.
3. a. Ran a four-person crew.
   b. Ran a crew.

## Practical English Skill 4: Proofread Your Résumé

**English Tip**
*A good résumé should be no more than one page long when typed.*

It is important to double-check the dates on your résumé. You need to **proofread** your résumé. Look for mistakes. Use a dictionary to check the spelling. Finally, have the résumé neatly typed. If you cannot type, there are services that will do this for you. A careless résumé full of mistakes will only turn an employer off.

## Practice

1. Use a dictionary to check the spelling of the words in this part of a résumé. Write the corrected paragraph on a separate piece of paper.

   Work Exprience: Short-order cook. Prepared and cookd an average of 60 meels per day. Supervized 4 waiters.

2. Write the second draft of your own résumé. Use action words and numbers. Be sure to check your spelling. Print it as neatly as you can on a piece of paper.

## Practical English Skill 5: Fill Out Job Applications

Many times, employers will ask you to fill out a job application. The application is a form much like a résumé. All you need to do is fill in the blanks. Here are some tips for filling out job applications.

1. Read over the application before you begin. Know exactly what you will be asked to include. Check to see if the application should be typed or printed.

2. Ask the employer if you can take the application home. At home, you can check spelling and take your time.

3. Ask for two applications in case you make a mistake. What if you have only one application? Practice filling in the information on another piece of paper. When you are happy with it, copy it onto the application.

4. Keep your résumé handy. Many times, you can simply copy information from your résumé to your application.

5. Proofread your application before you turn it in. Check spelling and dates one more time. Make sure you have filled in all the lines. See that all boxes are checked.

**Employment Application**

Date _____

| | |
|---|---|
| Name: | Phone No. |
| Address: | How long at this address: |
| Social Security #: | Are you a citizen of the U.S.: |
| Position for which you are applying: | Second Choice |
| Starting Salary Required: | Starting Salary Desired: |

Explain any health condition or physical handicap which could affect your ability to perform the type of work for which you are applying:

| | |
|---|---|
| How much time have you lost from work or school in the past two years: | Type of illness: |
| Our work schedule is 8:00 a.m. to 5:00 p.m., Monday—Friday. Are you able to conform to this work schedule? | What was the source of your referral to this company? |

Names of friends & relatives with this company:

In case of emergency, contact (name, address, phone #, relationship):

| **Education** | College | Other |
|---|---|---|
| Name of School | | |
| Address | | |
| Dates Attended | | |
| Grade Average | | |
| Major | | |
| Minor | | |

Are you studying now?

What?                                Where?

**For clerical personnel**
**Skills:**    Shorthand ( _____ WPM)        Typing ( _____ WPM)        Adding Machine (Touch:  Yes ☐  No ☐ )
           Others:

Have you ever served in a branch of the U.S. armed forces, and if so, please list branch of service, your rank, and dates of service:

To what professional, civic or social organizations do you belong (excluding those which indicate race, religion, or national origin)?

What are your principal hobbies?

| **Personal References:** Name | Address | Business | Years Acquainted |
|---|---|---|---|
| | | | |
| | | | |
| | | | |

**Practical English Tip**
*On a job application, you may see these words:*
For employer only. *Do not fill out the information in that section.*

*What information could you copy from your résumé onto this job application?*

## Practice

Write three tips for filling out a job application. Use a separate piece of paper.

### Your Social Security Number

Most job applications ask for your social security number. If you do not have a number, call your nearest Social Security Office. They will give you directions on how to get one. How do you find the Social Security Office? Look in the white pages of your phone book under the heading United States Government. Then look under the subheading "Health Education, and Welfare," or "Health and Human Services."

## Practical English Skill 6: Write a Cover Letter

**Dear ?**

*For a large company, you will often direct your letter to the personnel department. You can begin your letter with, "Dear Personnel Officer."*

It is a good idea to include a **cover letter** with your résumé or job application. The cover letter is a way to make your résumé more personal. A cover letter might include:

☐ The job title you are applying for

☐ Special skills not on your résumé

☐ Why you want to work for that company

Cover letters should always be short and to the point. Here is one example of a cover letter.

1622 University Avenue
Davis, CA 95616
April 7, 1995

Richard S. Garcia, D.V.M.
91 Walnut Street
Davis, CA 95616

Dear Dr. Garcia:

   Do you have an opening for a veterinary assistant? If you do, I would like to apply for the position.

   I will be graduating from high school in June, and I will then be available for full-time work. I grew up on a farm and have had experience raising and caring for farm animals and pets. Because I love animals, I would like to learn more about caring for them.

   I have included my résumé.

Sincerely,

*Carl Thomas*

Carl Thomas

---

## Practice

Write a cover letter to Personnel Department, Chicken & Chips, 1245 F Street, Boston, MA 34783. In the letter, ask if there are any management openings in your area. Mention that you are enclosing your résumé. In your cover letter, include anything else you think is important.

# Chapter Review

## Chapter Summary

- ☐ Résumés and job applications are your "foot in the door." They should be well-written and neat.

- ☐ A résumé usually has these parts: personal information, education, work experience, and skills.

- ☐ The purpose of the first draft of the résumé is to get information on paper. The second draft should include action verbs and words to measure your skills.

- ☐ Check spelling and dates on résumés and job applications.

- ☐ The cover letter is brief and to the point. It tells the reason you are writing.

## Putting Skills Together

Craig wants a "How-To" book on writing résumés. How would he find it in the library?

## Developing Writing Skills

Ask a friend or family member about his or her work experience, duties, and skills. Take notes and write the information in résumé form. Write a first draft and a second draft. Your second draft should include action words and words for measuring skills.

## Chapter Quiz

Use a separate piece of paper to answer these questions. Write one or two sentences in each answer.

1. What is a résumé? Why should it be neat?
2. What is the difference between a first draft and a second draft?
3. What are the five parts all résumés should include?
4. How can "action" words help a résumé?
5. Make this an "action" sentence? *I was the football coach's helper.*
6. How do numbers or measurements help a résumé?
7. Edit this item so that it includes a measurement: *Sewed clothes for school fashion show.*
8. How is a job application different from a résumé?
9. Why might you take a résumé with you when you plan to fill out a job application?
10. What three things might a cover letter include?

## Vocabulary Review

On a separate piece of paper, write the following sentences. Use the words in the box to fill in the blanks.

| résumé | accomplishment | duty | cover letter |
|---|---|---|---|

1. A _____ is often sent in with job applications and résumés.
2. A task performed on a job is a _____ .
3. A thing done well is an _____ .
4. A _____ is a written report of your work experience and skills.

# Chapter 9 Interviewing

*Speaking skills are important in job interviews. Employers like a person who has come prepared.*

## Chapter Learning Objectives

☐ Prepare questions and answers for interviews.

☐ Identify and practice techniques for speaking clearly.

☐ Identify and practice body language for interviews.

☐ Write a follow-up letter.

## Words to Know

**body language**    messages given by the body

**confident**    being sure of oneself

**co-workers**    fellow workers

**pronounce**    to say a word aloud

**role model**    a person you want to be like and learn from

**slang**    informal language that is not considered part of standard English

**visualization**    imagining

*Speak Up!*
*Employers like applicants with clear, strong voices. Do you speak clearly? Is that a skill you need to practice?*

Kim sits in front of a mirror. She takes a deep breath and smiles. Then she reads into a tape recorder. "I am a hard worker," she says. "I enjoy meeting people and solving problems. I think I would be very good in the Customer Service Department." Kim rewinds the tape recorder and plays back her words. "Not clear enough," she says. "Better try again."

Kim is getting ready for an interview. This chapter focuses on speaking skills and how they can help you in an interview.

## Practical English Skill 1: Prepare for Interviews

**Use Your Skills**

*Employers often begin an interview with, "Tell me about yourself." How would you prepare to answer this question?*

Suppose you are interviewing a person for a job. You ask a question. The person looks surprised. Then he starts to answer. "Uh, uh, well, I don't know," he says.

Employers want people who are prepared to talk about themselves. Some questions that employers ask are easy to prepare for. For example:

☐   Will you take part-time work?

☐   Do you have experience in this field?

☐   How will you get to work every day?

Other questions require more thought. You should be ready to answer them. Before you go to an interview, ask yourself these five questions. Then *write* the answers on a piece of paper.

1. Why do you want to work here?

Employers want someone who will be part of the team. They want someone who *wants* to work for them. To prepare, you might ask other workers what they like about the company. Or tell the employer what you think it would be like to work there.

2. What are your strengths?

Before the interview, write down three of your strengths. Think of your skills and the things people like about you. Be matter of fact. Don't be shy, and don't brag. If you are skilled at typing, say so. If people like working with you, admit it.

3. What are your weaknesses?

Think of three weaknesses that can also be strengths. For example, you may be easily bothered by lazy **co-workers.** This could mean you are a hard worker yourself. A weakness could also be something you haven't learned yet. But you can simply tell the employer you are ready and willing to learn. Employers can think of this weakness as a strength.

4. Why should we hire you instead of someone else?

Restate your skills and your willingness to work. Employers want to know that you are **confident.**

5. Why did you leave your other jobs?

Here, you should be honest and positive. Perhaps you wanted more money, or you didn't like the work. If you were fired, explain why. Never speak badly of your former employers.

---

## Practice

Do the following work on a separate piece of paper.

1. Think of a company you would like to work for. List three reasons that the company appeals to you.

2. List three of your strengths and three weaknesses. Use weaknesses that can also be seen as strengths.

3. Imagine that you were fired from your last job. You didn't get along with your boss. Write how you will answer the question: *Why did you leave your last job?*

## Practical English Skill 2: Pronounce Words Clearly

Turn on the radio. Listen to the news. Can you understand every word? Do you hear **slang**? Slang is informal language that is not considered part of standard English. Does the person sound relaxed?

**Synonyms for Slang**
*Synonyms are words with similar meanings. What are synonyms for some of the slang words you use?*

The radio news announcer is a good **role model** for clear speech. In an interview, you should **pronounce** every word clearly. Speak loudly enough to be heard—but not so loudly that you are shouting. You want to be matter of fact and pleasant. Do not be overly friendly, either. Remember you are there on business.

You can do several things to improve your speech:

☐ Practice your interview answers in front of a mirror. Watch your mouth as you pronounce each word. Use your facial muscles and lips to say words clearly.

☐ Take a deep breath before you speak. This will relax you and give strength to your voice.

☐ Speak into a tape recorder. Play it back and listen to yourself. What sounds good? How can you improve?

☐ Act out the interview with a friend. Get to the point where you do not need your notes. Accept what your friend has to say about your speech, and then work to improve it.

## Practice

1. Feel your face muscles, lips, and tongue move as you say these words? *I am going to Iowa to practice my speech.*

2. Have a classmate act as the job interviewer. Tell the person about your strengths.

3. Ask your classmate for feedback on these things:

☐ clearness of words

☐ strength of your voice

☐ how relaxed you sound

4. On a separate piece of paper, write two things you do well. Write two things you need to improve.

**A Word About Slang**

Interviewers like to hear standard grammar without slang. Which is better for an interview: "I ain't that kind of dude" or "I am not that kind of person"?

## Practical English Skill 3: Use Body Language Effectively

Sally thought she was all prepared for an interview. She had practiced speaking. Her voice and words were clear and true. But during the interview, she stared at the employer's desk. It really didn't matter what she said. Her eyes said that she was scared.

Using the right **body language** is so important it is actually a speaking skill. Here are some do's and don'ts for body language.

☐ Do make eye contact. Don't stare.

☐ Do smile occasionally. Don't grin or frown.

☐ Do nod your head up and down thoughtfully. Don't look away.

☐  Do use your hands in an open, friendly way. Don't point, cross your arms, or wring your hands together.

☐  Do sit tall. Don't slouch.

☐  Do keep your feet on the floor and your legs together. Don't shake your feet.

## Practice

List the do's of body language on a separate piece of paper. Then practice one of your interview questions in front of a mirror. Check to make sure you are following each of the "do's."

### See It in Your Head

Before a big match, some tennis players imagine the game. In their minds they "see" their perfect strokes. They return serves with power. They win the game.

Seeing success in your head is called **visualization.** Visualization can help you be more confident. And it is a simple, quiet way to prepare. To visualize, just close your eyes. Take a deep breath. See your relaxed smile. Hear your clear voice. Be impressed by your great answers. At the real interview, those practical English skills you visualized will be easier to act out.

## Practical English Skill 4: Write a Follow-Up Letter

What do you do when you have completed the interview process? First, it is a good idea to write a follow-up letter to the person who interviewed you.

In this letter, you should restate your interest in the position. And you should thank the person for the time he or she took to interview you. Be sure to spell the interviewer's name and the company's name correctly. Also, be sure that you write the address of the company or store correctly.

Study this example:

463 Oak Avenue
San Pedro, CA 90733
July 18, 1995

Paulette Davis
Personnel Director
Tiny Tot Day-Care Center
1982 Parker Drive
San Mateo, CA  94403

Dear Ms. Davis:

Thank you for the time you spent interviewing me on July 17. I would like to tell you again how interested I am in working for Tiny Tot Day-Care Center. I believe that my experience in the field of child care qualifies me for the position that is open.

Sincerely,

*Sharon Martin*

Sharon Martin

## Practice

On a separate piece of paper, write a follow-up letter. Use correct business letter form. Follow the style of the example.

# Chapter Review

## Chapter Summary

- ☐ Speaking skills are important in job interviews. Interviewers like a person who has come prepared.

- ☐ Write the answers to questions that might be asked.

- ☐ Interviewers like clear, strong speech.

- ☐ Body language is just as important as what you say. Sit tall, keep your chin up, and make eye contact.

- ☐ It is important to write a follow-up letter after an interview.

## Putting Skills Together

The interview is also a time for you to ask questions. Write four questions you could ask in a job interview. Example: "If I do my job well, what kind of future do I have here?"

## Developing Writing Skills

Saul is interviewing at a bank. He wants to be a bank teller. He likes people, and he is good at math. He also wants to learn how to use computers. In past jobs, people have complained that he is too fussy and neat.

The job interviewer asks Saul, "Why should I hire you instead of someone else?" Write down what Saul might say.

## Chapter Quiz

Use a separate piece of paper to answer these questions. Write one or two sentences in each answer.

1. Why is it important to prepare for an interview?
2. What are the five questions you should prepare for?
3. Give an example of a weakness that could be seen as a strength. Explain.
4. When asked why he left his last job, Jim said, "I couldn't stand that place. It was dirty. There were bugs everywhere." What did he do wrong?
5. How could Jim have answered in a more positive way?
6. How should your voice and words sound when you speak?
7. What is one good way to practice speaking?
8. What are two "do's" for body language?
9. What are two "don'ts" for body language?
10. How can visualization help you prepare for an interview?

## Vocabulary Review

Match the words on the left to their meanings on the right. Write the numbers and letters on a separate piece of paper.

1. co-workers           a. messages given by the body
2. confident            b. informal language
3. pronounce            c. being sure of oneself
4. slang                d. fellow workers
5. body language        e. to say a word aloud
6. role model           f. imagining
7. visualization        g. a person you want to be like

*After finishing the paperwork, it's time to start learning your new job duties. A senior employee usually shows you around and shows you how things are done.*

## Chapter Learning Objectives

☐ List three kinds of information found in employee handbooks.

☐ Use the table of contents to see what is covered in the employee handbook.

☐ Identify two ways the index and glossary of the employee handbook can be used.

☐ Name two tips for filling out forms.

☐ List three key words used on paycheck stubs.

## Words to Know

**acronym**   an abbreviation based on first letters of words in a title or slogan, as BART for Bay Area Rapid Transit

**benefits**   extras, such as health insurance, for workers

**deductions**   money taken from a paycheck for taxes and other things

**personnel department**   a company department that hires employees and helps them solve problems

**policies**   a company's rules

**Statement of Earnings and Deductions**   part of a paycheck stub telling how much money was earned and how much was deducted

**If It Were You**

*What would you do if you were Sara? Where would you begin?*

It is Sara's first day on the job. She is the new receptionist. The boss places a big book on Sara's desk. "Here," she says. "I don't have time to go over this with you today. Get to know the company first." Then she walks away.

For a minute, Sara feels like walking away, too. Instead, she uses her English skills to learn more about her job. This chapter will help you build those same skills.

## Practical English Skill 1: Study the Employee Handbook

The big book Sara's boss gave her was the employee handbook. Many times, these books look big and unfriendly. But they can give you important information about the company you are working for. Most often, they contain information about these things:

☐ **The company's policies. Policies** are the "do's and don'ts" you need to know. Companies often have policies about what you should wear to work. They have policies about being late and taking breaks. They might even have a policy about having food at your desk. Knowing policies can help save you from embarrassing moments. It can help you be comfortable on the job.

☐ **Worker benefits.** Most companies offer some kind of **benefits** to their workers. The employee handbook can explain these benefits to you. For example, your company may offer you a choice of health plans. The employee handbook could tell what the plans are and how to sign up for them.

☐ **The company departments and what they do.** A large company can have many departments. Knowing these departments and what they do can make your life simpler. For example, suppose you have questions about health plans. You could look to see if the company has a **personnel department.** The people there help workers with questions about overtime or missed paychecks. They can also answer health plan questions and tell you what to do about other common problems.

### Practice

Imagine that tomorrow is Halloween. You are thinking about dressing up like a clown and going to work. Can the employee handbook help you decide if this is a good idea? Explain your answer on a separate piece of paper.

## Practical English Skill 2: Use the Employee Handbook

*English on the Job*
*When could you find the time to study the employee handbook?*

Employee handbooks are often very large books. Knowing where and how to begin is your first problem. The table of contents can help you. First, look over the table of contents. Read the chapters that are most important to you first. And, of course, take notes to remember key information. You can wait until later to read sections of the handbook that are least important to you.

### Practice

Do the following exercise on a separate piece of paper.

It is your first day on the job. You open up your Employee Handbook. This is what you see first:

Table of Contents
I.     Your First Day on the Job
II.    Choosing a Health Plan
III.   History of the Company
IV.   Opportunities
V.    Your Work Review
VI.   Sick Leave and Holidays
VII.  All About Pay

Remember, it is your first day on the job. You have been told that you do not have to sign up for a health plan for ninety days. You also have been told that you will have your first work review after the first ninety days.

*What if you left your handbook at home? If you need a quick answer you can always ask a co-worker to help you.*

Read the sections of the table of contents. Put them in the order in which they are important to you. Explain why you put them in that order.

### Finding Key Information

Suppose you work at a fast food restaurant. This restaurant has rules for everything. Before your first shift, you want to quickly review how to greet customers.

Remember, you can quickly find such information by using the index. Simply look up "greeting customers" in the back of the book. You will probably find an entry.

### Special Words on the Job

It is your third week on the job. Your boss comes up to you and says, "Fill out a STAR report." Then she disappears. You don't know what a STAR report is. How can you find out?

**Work Vocabulary**
*If you work now, think of special words you use only at work. How did you learn their meanings?*

You will often have to learn special words for doing your job. When you need help with these words, look in the glossary or index of your employee handbook. STAR is probably an **acronym**—a group of letters that stand for words. For example, STAR could stand for South Texas Account Report. By using the employee handbook, you can find out what STAR is and how to fill out a STAR report.

## Practice

Answer the following questions about the employee handbook on a separate piece of paper.

1. What are three reasons to read the employee handbook?

2. Your boss tells you to talk to the PPO. Where could you find what PPO stands for?

3. You want to know if life insurance is offered by the company. To find out, where in the index could you look?

## Practical English Skill 3: Fill Out Forms

Today's work world is filled with papers, reports, and computers. During your first week on the job, you will probably have to fill out a few forms. Such forms help a company keep track of who you are and what you should be paid.  For example, look at the W-4 form on page 124. This form helps your employer know how much in taxes to keep out of your paycheck.

At first look, the W-4 is confusing. Here are some English skills to help you fill out the W-4 and other such forms.

☐  Read the entire form before you fill it out.

☐  Make a list of words or directions that you do not understand.

☐  Go to your supervisor or the personnel department where you work. Get the answers to your questions. Don't feel embarrassed about asking these questions. You are new on the job. Asking questions is a sign that you are willing and able to learn.

☐ Fill out the form neatly.

☐ Have your supervisor or the personnel department check it over.

☐ Turn the form in on time.

---

-------------------- **Cut here and give the certificate to your employer. Keep the top portion for your records.** --------------------

| Form **W-4** Department of the Treasury Internal Revenue Service | **Employee's Withholding Allowance Certificate** ▶ **For Privacy Act and Paperwork Reduction Act Notice, see reverse.** | OMB No. 1545-0010 **1993** |
|---|---|---|

| 1 Type or print your first name and middle initial | Last name | 2 Your social security number |
|---|---|---|

| Home address (number and street or rural route) | 3 ☐ Single ☐ Married ☐ Married, but withhold at higher Single rate. **Note:** *If married, but legally separated, or spouse is a nonresident alien, check the Single box.* |
|---|---|
| City or town, state, and ZIP code | 4 If your last name differs from that on your social security card, check here and call 1-800-772-1213 for more information · · · ▶ ☐ |

5   Total number of allowances you are claiming (from line G above or from the worksheets on page 2 if they apply) .   **5**
6   Additional amount, if any, you want withheld from each paycheck . . . . . . . . . . .   **6** $
7   I claim exemption from withholding for 1993 and I certify that I meet **ALL** of the following conditions for exemption:
   ● Last year I had a right to a refund of **ALL** Federal income tax withheld because I had **NO** tax liability; **AND**
   ● This year I expect a refund of **ALL** Federal income tax withheld because I expect to have **NO** tax liability; **AND**
   ● This year if my income exceeds $600 and includes nonwage income, another person cannot claim me as a dependent.
   If you meet all of the above conditions, enter "EXEMPT" here · · · · · · · · · · ▶   **7**

Under penalties of perjury, I certify that I am entitled to the number of withholding allowances claimed on this certificate or entitled to claim exempt status.

Employee's signature ▶                                        Date ▶                              , 19

| 8 Employer's name and address (Employer: Complete 8 and 10 only if sending to the IRS) | 9 Office code (optional) | 10 Employer identification number |
|---|---|---|

Cat. No. 10220Q

### Practice

Answer the following questions on a separate piece of paper.

1. Look at the W-4 form "Personal Allowances Worksheet." Imagine that you are going to fill it out. Make a list of the words you do not know.

2. Look over the directions. Write any questions you have about filling out the form.

3. Who might have the answers to your questions?

## Practical English Skill 4: Interpret Your Paycheck Stub

Finally, payday comes. You are handed a paycheck. Attached to it is your paycheck stub. This is called a **Statement of Earnings and Deductions**. You should read the paycheck stub carefully to make sure you are getting the right amount of money. It shows these things:

☐ How much money you earned (gross pay)

☐ What **deductions** were taken from your earned pay

☐ Your take-home pay (net pay)

Look at the sample paycheck stub on page 126.

**CORVALIS SHIPPING CENTER**                                    LENOX MILL, OH

| EMPLOYEE NUMBER | CURRENT HOURS | | YEAR TO DATE | | | | | |
|---|---|---|---|---|---|---|---|---|
| | REGULAR | OVERTIME | Y.T.D. GROSS | F.I.T. | F.I.C.A. | LOCAL | STATE | RET. |
| 017338 | 29 50 | 00 | 1115 25 | 71 70 | 65 24 | 11 16 | 22 31 | 9 29 |

| CURRENT EARNINGS | | | CURRENT | | | | | |
|---|---|---|---|---|---|---|---|---|
| REGULAR | OVERTIME | SPECIAL | CURRENT GROSS | F.I.T. | F.I.C.A. | LOCAL | STATE | RET. |
| 177 00 | 00 | 00 | 177 00 | 13 77 | 10 35 | 1 77 | 3 54 | 9 29 |

| CHECK NO. | DESCRIPTION | AMOUNT | DESCRIPTION | AMOUNT | TOTAL DEDUCTIONS |
|---|---|---|---|---|---|
| 046790 | | | | | 38 72 |

ENDING DATE
09 03 90

138 28
NET PAY

CHECK DATE
09 03 90

AUTHORIZED DEDUCTIONS AND SPECIAL PAY ELEMENTS

STATEMENT OF EARNINGS AND DEDUCTIONS • DETACH AND RETAIN FOR YOUR RECORDS

At first, you might be confused by so much information. Here's how to make sense of a paycheck stub:

1. Look at each box or section as one piece of information.

2. Read each piece of information carefully.

3. Make a list of questions.

4. Go to a co-worker, your supervisor, or the personnel department to get your questions answered.

**Vocabulary for Reading Your Paycheck Stub**

Your paycheck stub has its own language. Here is a list of words, abbreviations, and their meanings to help you out.

| | |
|---|---|
| **Pay period:** | Time period for which you are being paid |
| **Gross pay:** | The total amount of money you earned in the pay period |
| **Y.T.D.:** | year-to-date |
| **Net pay:** | How much you've earned after all deductions. This is your take-home pay. It is the actual amount of money your check is worth. |
| **F.I.T.:** | Federal income tax |
| **F.I.C.A.:** | Social security tax; the letters stand for Federal Insurance Contribution Act |
| **Local:** | Local taxes such as county or city |
| **State:** | State taxes |
| **Ret.:** | Retirement fund |
| **Regular:** | Hours or pay at your usual rate |
| **Overtime:** | Hours or pay over your usual rate |

## Practice

Use the vocabulary list above to answer the following questions about the paycheck stub on page 126. Write your answers on a separate piece of paper.

1. How much social security tax was taken out of the person's pay?
2. Did the person work any overtime hours?
3. What is the person's gross pay for the pay period?
4. How much has the person earned this year?
5. After all deductions, what is the person's net pay?

# Chapter Review

---

## Chapter Summary

- ☐ Most employee handbooks contain information about worker benefits and company policies.

- ☐ Look over the chapters in the employee handbook to find the information that is most important to you.

- ☐ Use the index and glossary of the employee handbook to find key information and learn special words.

- ☐ To fill out forms carefully, read through them first. Make notes about words and directions before you fill the forms out. Ask co-workers, supervisors, or the personnel department for help.

- ☐ Read paycheck stubs carefully. Look at each piece of information and learn what it means.

## Putting Skills Together

Do you think a dictionary could help you read a paycheck stub? Explain your answer.

## Developing Writing Skills

On a separate piece of paper, finish the paragraph below. Use what you learned in this chapter and through your own experiences. Write at least five sentencnes.

*You may be nervous on your first day of work. But there are a few things you can do to make things go smoothly. Begin by . . .*

## Chapter Quiz

Use a separate piece of paper to answer these questions. Write one or two sentences in each answer.

1. What are three things usually contained in an employee handbook?

2. What is the first thing you should do with the employee handbook?

3. Give an example of how you might use the index of an employee handbook.

4. Your boss tells you to check with the RRD. How could you use the employee handbook to help you find out what the RRD is?

5. Why might you take notes when you read the employee handbook?

6. What is a common form you will need to fill out at work?

7. If you are confused when you look at a form, what should you do?

8. Why is it important to read the Statement of Earnings and Deductions?

9. What is the difference between gross pay and net pay?

10. What does F.I.C.A. stand for?

## Vocabulary Review

On a separate piece of paper, write three sentences of your own. Use at least one of these vocabulary words in each of your sentences.

policies                    benefits                    deductions

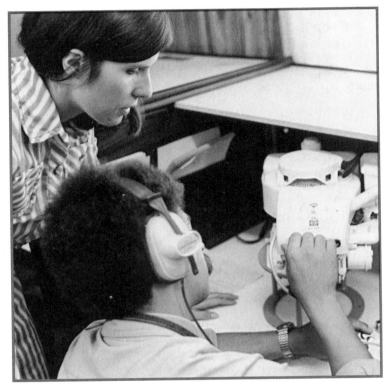

*Learning difficult job skills takes effort and patience. It also helps to use job aids like charts and step-by-step instructions.*

## Chapter Learning Objectives

☐ Tell what a job aid is.

☐ List the steps for using job aids.

☐ Name three common types of job aids.

☐ Write or make a job aid.

## Words to Know

**job aid**   anything that helps a person do his or her job efficiently

**procedure**   the steps in which a task is accomplished

**promotion**   advancement to a job with more responsibility

**task**   small part of a large job

Jerry just got a **promotion.** He has the new responsibility of opening up the restaurant in the morning. His supervisor leads him through the steps.

*How does a boss choose which person should get a promotion?*

"First you turn off the alarm. You put in this key, turn it, and punch in the code X12238. If you get it wrong, call 555-9000 and give them this code number:  990002. That's your secret code number. It lets the alarm company know you are not a thief. If you don't have it, watch out. The police will be here in minutes."

Is Jerry lost? Does he have to remember all this new information the first time he hears it? Of course not. He uses his English skills to learn new job skills. He knows how to write and use **job aids**.

## Practical English Skill 1: Use Job Aids

A job aid is anything that helps you learn or do your job correctly. Job aids can be forms, lists of steps, instructions, manuals, and so on. Here are three examples of common job aids and how to use them:

### The Telephone Message Form

This job aid tells you the key information to get from a person when you are taking a message. A sample telephone job aid is shown below.

```
TO _____

DATE _____  TIME _____

                  WHILE YOU WERE OUT
                  YOU WERE CALLED
BY _____

FROM _____

HIS/HER PHONE NUMBER _____

                      MESSAGE
_____
_____
_____
_____

MESSAGE TAKEN BY _____
```

To use this job aid, keep it in front of you when you answer the phone. Get the key information you need from the caller: his or her name, phone number, the message, and where the caller is from. Fill in the rest of the information as soon as you hang up: the date, time, and your name. This saves you and the caller time on the phone.

## The Work Schedule

In some types of jobs, your hours could change from week to week. In such cases, work schedules are posted to let you know your weekly shifts. Often, these job aids are in chart form. To read them, simply use your skills from Chapter 1. Here is an example.

|            | M | T | W | Th | F |
|------------|---|---|---|----|---|
| Abrams, J. | 8—1<br>AM PM | 8—1<br>AM PM | 12—5<br>AM PM | 8—1<br>AM PM | 12—5<br>AM PM |
| Kelly, M.  | 12—5<br>PM PM | 12—5<br>PM PM | 8—1<br>AM PM | 4—8<br>PM PM | 4—8<br>PM PM |
| Scott, C.  | 6—10<br>PM PM | 6—10<br>PM PM | 6—10<br>PM PM | 12—5<br>PM PM | 8—1<br>AM PM |

*You can see that J. Abrams is working from 12 to 5 on Wednesday.*

## The "How To" Job Aid

*Everyday English*
*Think of job aids you use to operate machines in your home.*

The "How To" job aid is a list of step-by-step instructions. Perhaps it tells you an office **procedure** or how to run a machine. Usually, these instructions are written. Here is an example of a "how to" job aid found in a small business office.

### Closing Procedures

1. Check to see that all computers and typewriters are off.
2. Turn on answering machine.
3. Close drapes.
4. Turn on alarm.
5. Shut off lights.
6. Lock the door.

Such job aids are usually simple to follow. You just have to read and carry out the steps one by one.

## Practice

Use a separate piece of paper to answer these questions.

1. What might happen if you waited to fill out the telephone message form until after you hung up the phone?

2. Look at the work schedule on page 133. If you were Mary Kelly, what hours would you work on Wednesday?

3. Suppose you want an evening shift on Wednesday. Which person(s) might you ask to switch with you?

## Practical English Skill 2: Make Your Own Job Aid

Remember Jerry at the beginning of the chapter? His boss didn't give him a job aid for opening up the restaurant. So he decided to make one. This is what it looked like:

### Opening

1. Put in alarm key and turn.

2. Punch code X12238.

Alarm Company: 555-9000

My code: 990002

*What could happen if everyone knew the secret alarm codes?*

Jerry kept this job aid in his wallet. That way, no one else could see the secret codes.

Many times when you are learning job skills, people will tell you how to do something. But it can be hard to remember all these steps after hearing them just once. To make your own job aid, you should:

1. Listen carefully for each step of how to perform a **task**.

2. Write the steps down in order.

3. Include any other important information on the job aid.

4. Put the job aid in a place where it is easy to use.

## Practice

Make a job aid out of these instructions.

"You're going to have to learn how to file these reports. It's really easy. Just look for the report name. You can find it on the top right of the report cover. Well, sometimes it's at the bottom. Then file the reports alphabetically. Don't forget to take out the yellow sheet in each report first. Take the yellow sheets marked 'Yes' to Shipping. Put the yellow sheets marked 'No' in the trash can."

# Chapter Review

## Chapter Summary

☐ A job aid is anything you can use to help you learn and remember job skills.

☐ Common job aids are forms, charts, and "how to" instructions.

☐ Making a job aid is a good way to learn skills on the job.

☐ Job aids should include step-by-step instructions. They should include key information on how to do a task.

## Putting Skills Together

Is listening an important skill for every worker? Explain your answer.

## Developing Writing Skills

Suppose you are going out of town. You have hired someone to take care of your house or apartment. Write a short job aid on how to do one important task while you are gone. (Examples: Feeding the dog, locking up.)

## Chapter Quiz

Use a separate piece of paper to answer these questions. Write one or two sentences in each answer.

1. What is a job aid?

2. Explain how a telephone message form is a job aid.

3. What kinds of information do you usually take while a caller is on the phone?

4. What kinds of information do you usually fill in after the caller has hung up?

5. Explain why a work schedule is a job aid.

6. What are "how to" job aids?

7. Give two examples of "how to" job aids.

8. What do "how to" job aids usually include?

9. Why is it a good idea to carry a paper and pencil with you while you are learning your job?

10. Why should job aids be easy to use?

## Vocabulary Review

Match the words on the left to their meanings on the right. Write the numbers and corresponding letters on a separate piece of paper.

1. promotion    a. small part of a large job

2. job aid    b. the steps in which a task is accomplished

3. task    c. advancement to a job with more responsibility

4. procedure    d. anything that helps a person do a job

# Chapter *12* Communicating at Work

*Good customer service requires good communication skills. Who else do you have to communicate with when you're on the job?*

## Chapter Learning Objectives

- ☐ Identify three ways to communicate on the job.
- ☐ Write an outline of a business message.
- ☐ List at least three rules for good business writing.
- ☐ Identify two ways to deal with angry customers.

## Words to Know

**communication**   giving and receiving information

**memo**   short note

**presentation**   the act of showing or explaining something to another person or group

**topic sentence**   a sentence that introduces the subject or states the purpose

**Communication** is the giving and receiving of information. You communicate daily with family and friends. When communication breaks down, there can be misunderstandings. Things don't get done. Feelings get hurt.

Communication is just as important on the job. Just suppose

- [ ] Your co-worker is not doing his or her share of work. How do let your co-worker know how you feel about it?

- [ ] You think your boss is treating you unfairly. How do you present your case?

- [ ] You have a great idea. How do you get people to listen to you?

- [ ] There has been a change in procedures. How do you let everyone know?

## Practical English Skill 1: Communicate on the Job

There are many ways of communicating on the job. Take the case of the problem co-worker or the unfair boss. It might be best to speak to the person face to face. But if nothing changes, you would probably want to put your side of the story in writing. You would need to write a report stating the facts.

**Words in the Workplace**
*Does the word* memo *sound like the word memory? Why do you think this is so?*

Now suppose you just want to tell your ideas to the boss. You could make a **presentation** in person or in writing. And what if you need to get information to your co-workers? Just write a **memo.** A memo is a short note to co-workers.

### The Employee Handbook and Communication

Many times, companies have formal procedures for solving employee problems. It is a good idea to look these procedures up in the employee handbook.

### Practice

Use a separate piece of paper to answer these questions.

1. What problems do you think could be caused by poor communication on the job?

2. How could good communication improve a workplace?

3. What are three ways to communicate on the job?

## Practical English Skill 2: Use an Outline

Whether you are planning to communicate in person or in writing, you must prepare. One of the best ways to prepare is by starting with an outline.

Most of the time, this is the type of outline you will use:

I.    Topic sentence

The **topic sentence** tells the reason you are writing (or speaking).

II.    Supporting Sentences or Body

    A.

    B.

    C.

Supporting sentences are the facts that "hold up" the topic sentence. The body contains the important information.

III.    Closing Sentence(s)

This tops off your presentation. Your closing sentences could tell what you want the outcome of your presentation to be. Or you might thank people for reading or listening to your ideas.

Here is an example of such an outline. The writer, Louis, is going to make his presentation in person to his boss. But he is preparing his ideas on paper.

I.    I want to suggest ways to improve the office.

II.    My ideas are as follows:

    A. Move the receptionist and phone to the far wall. This will keep the rest of the office quieter. Workers will be able to concentrate better.

B.   Move the copy machine into the back room. This will give us more room for files. It will also keep the front office quieter.

III.   Thank you for listening.

Notice Louis's supporting sentences. He tells exactly how his suggestions will improve the office. And he doesn't let his feelings get in the way. Suppose he had written: *It is too noisy in that front office. Nobody can work. If you don't quiet it down, I'll quit and so will everybody else.* He's being very negative, and sounds angry. His boss might just invite him to quit.

## Practice

**Use Your Body Language**
*Look back at Chapter 9. Review the body language you used in interviews. Should this body language be used in all kinds of spoken communication? Explain.*

Andre is busing tables at a busy restaurant. His co-worker is just not doing his share. For four days in a row, Andre has had to clean tables in his co-worker's section. In addition, Andre has had to sweep both sections twice this week. Yet they split tips down the middle. Andre would like his co-worker to get busy and do his share. He is feeling angry about the situation.

On a separate piece of paper, prepare an outline of what Andre might say to his co-worker. Keep feelings out of it. Stick to the facts.

## Practical English Skill 3: Put It on Paper

You may choose to communicate by memo, by letter, or in some other written form. Suppose Louis's boss took his suggestions. The boss might put out a memo that looks like this:

To: Office Staff
From: Mr. Davis
Regarding: Changes in the Office

There will be some changes  happening in the front office next week.

1.  The receptionist and phone will be moving to the far wall.

2.  The copy machine will be moved to the back room. These changes will make the front office quieter.

Thanks for the suggestions.

**Saying Good-Bye**

*When you decide to leave a job, write a letter of resignation. State that you are leaving and tell what your final day will be. It is fine to include the reasons you are moving on. But make sure you don't leave any hard feelings behind.*

The memo follows rules of good business writing. The writing is to the point. The words are simple. Good business writing should save the readers' time and be understandable. Long words and sentences can get in the way of the meaning.

Whenever you are writing on the job, follow these rules:

### Rules for Writing on the Job

1.  Write an outline, a first draft, and a final draft.

2.  Use a topic sentence, supporting sentences, and a closing.

3.  Write your drafts in short, complete sentences.

4.  Stick to the facts that matter. Don't carry on about your feelings.

5.  Always remember to check your spelling. Use a dictionary.

## Practice

Here is an accident report. Write a final draft of the report on a separate piece of paper. Use the rules for writing on page 143.

This is a report of the accident that happened on June 18th. It was terrible. I was standing by the loading dock. A truck pulled in. I was drinking coffee. Hey! A guy needs to relax. Anyway, a truck pulled in when I wasn't looking. The truck bumped a stack of boxes on the dock. One box fell on my foot. My co-worker, Jack Smith, called for help right away. Jack's a great guy. I was taken to Mount Eden Hospital and treated for a broken foot. What bad luck!

## When You're Treated Unfairly

*Is all discrimination about race? Are people ever treated unfairly because of their age or sex?*

Suppose you believe you are being discriminated against on your job. You can't seem to solve the problem. Write a letter to the Equal Employment Opportunity Commission, 2401 E Street NW, Washington, DC 20507. If you wish to call, dial 800-USA-EEOC.

## Practical English Skill 4: Communicate with Customers

Marcia is a salesperson in a music store. A customer comes in. He slams a compact disc down on the counter. "You people are crooks," he screams at Marcia. "This stupid CD skips. I ought to turn you in to the Better Business Bureau."

Marcia should:

a. start to cry.

b. refuse to talk to him.

c. take a deep breath and say, " Let's see if we can solve this problem."

If you chose c, you already understand the first step in working with customers. Most of the time, it is easy to communicate with customers. You find out what they want. You try to be helpful. You smile and do your job well.

**English Manners**
*How could chewing gum on the job get in the way of communicating with a customer?*

But with an angry customer, you must use all your skills as a good communicator. Don't take the customer's anger personally. The customer is not really angry with you. He or she is angry about something that happened.

If you start shouting back, the problem will only get worse. If you cry or talk softly, you will not be doing your job. Stay calm. Nod your head to show that you are listening to the customer. Talk in a clear, strong voice. Always stay focused on solving the problem. If the situation gets out of hand, get your boss or another co-worker to help you.

## Practice

Use a separate piece of paper to answer these questions.

1. What are three jobs in which you might deal with customers?

2. What kind of body language should you use with customers?

3. What is the best way to handle an angry customer?

# Chapter Review

## Chapter Summary

- ☐ Communicating takes place all the time on the job. Being a good communicator can help solve problems and make your job easier.

- ☐ Outlines help prepare you for written or spoken communication. The outline should have a topic sentence, supporting sentences, and a closing.

- ☐ Most business writing should be short and to the point. Use complete sentences, easy words, and check spelling on final drafts. Talk about facts, not feelings.

- ☐ Communicating with customers is a skill. Always stay calm, open, and friendly—even with angry customers.

## Putting Skills Together

Many times, companies have policies about how you should communicate with customers. How could you find out about this policy?

## Developing Writing Skills

Imagine that you are going to ask your boss for a raise. Make an outline. Include at least three reasons that you deserve the raise. Then write out the presentation.

## Chapter Quiz

Use a separate piece of paper to answer these questions. Write one or two sentences in each answer.

1. What is communication?

2. Write an example of a topic sentence.

3. Write two supporting sentences for the topic sentence in number 2.

4. Write a closing sentence to complete your outline.

5. Why is it good to write an outline before you give a presentation in person?

6. What is a memo?

7. The company baseball team is practicing on Tuesday at 7:00 p.m. instead of Thursday at 8:00 p.m. Write a memo to your co-workers about this change.

8. Which is better business writing: being short and to the point, or using long words and sentences? Explain.

9. What are three things you should do when communicating with an angry customer?

## Vocabulary Review

Match the words on the left to their meanings on the right. Write the numbers and corresponding letters on a separate piece of paper.

1. communication

2. presentation

3. topic sentence

a. a sentence that introduces the subject or states the purpose

b. giving and receiving information

c. the act of showing or explaining ideas to another person or group.

# Unit Review

1. Do you think a person's job goals and interests always stay the same? Ten years from now, how might your goals be different? Explain your thinking?

2. Compare a private employment agency and the state department of employment. Name one similarity and one difference.

3. How do you get a Social Security number?

4. Why is it a good idea to ask an employer for two job applications?

5. Suppose an employer asks why you were fired from your last job. Should you say it was a terrible company to work for? Why or why not?

6. Why should you practice interviewing with a friend before going out on a real job interview? Name two ways that can help you.

7. What does your W-4 form tell your employer?

8. Where will employees find their Statement of Earnings and Deductions?

9. Think of a job task you know how to do. Write at least three step-by-step procedures for getting that task done.

10. What job aid tells you if you have to work next Wednesday? What job aid could show you how to add paper to the copying machine?

11. Write two supporting sentences for the following topic sentence. *Something has to be done about the food in the cafeteria.*

12. How is a memo different from a presentation? Explain your answer.

# Unit Four

# English for Independent Living

# Chapter *13* Finding a Place to Live

How can you find a nice apartment at the right price? The rental ads in the newspaper are a good place to begin looking.

## Chapter Learning Objectives

- [ ] Use lists of pros and cons to compare different living situations.
- [ ] Find key information in rental ads.
- [ ] Write an interview guide for landlords.
- [ ] Fill out a rental application.
- [ ] Find key words and phrases in a lease.

## Words to Know

**credit reference**   person or business who can vouch that a person pays his or her bills

**landlord**   person who owns rental property

**lease**   written contract between landlord and tenant

**not applicable**   does not apply

**obligated**   having responsibility for something

**personal reference**   person who can vouch for a person's good character

**refundable deposit**   money that can be returned if certain conditions are met

**tenant**   renter

**utilities**   gas, electricity, and water

**vouch**   to speak in favor of; to say that something is true

Dee and Leo are having tea in Dee's new apartment.

"Wow," says Leo. "This place is nice."

Dee frowns. "Yes, at first glance I thought so, too. But the neighborhood is dangerous. The neighbors are noisy. And I have to walk a long way to catch the bus. I wish I'd looked closer before I moved in."

Don't let this happen to you. Use the practical English skills in this chapter to find a good place to live.

## Practical English Skill 1: List Pros and Cons of Living Situations

At one time, the American dream was to grow up, get a job, and buy a house. But in today's housing market, fewer people can afford to buy. More people are finding they must choose to

☐  Rent an apartment on their own

☐  Rent an apartment and share it with roommates

☐  Rent a room in a house and share the kitchen

There are pros and cons to each of these situations. Use your English skills to outline them. Here is a list of one person's pros and cons for renting an apartment without roommates.

**Use Your Skills**

*How could you use lists of pros and cons after you start looking for a place to live?*

### Pros

1. Privacy

2. Don't have to clean up other people's messes

3. Don't have to worry about roommates not paying bills

### Cons

1. Can get lonely

2. Have to pay all the bills myself

3. No one to feed my cat when I'm out of town

Listing the pros and cons lets you make a comparison. You can then make a decision based on your values. You might decide that roommates are too much trouble. You might decide that you'll work things out with a roommate to have company and save money.

### Practice

On a separate piece of paper, list at least three pros and cons for each of the three living situations listed on page 152. Then decide which arrangement best suits your needs.

## Practical English Skill 2: Read Rental Ads

**Use Your Skills**

*How could you use lists of pros and cons to decide which neighborhood is best for you?*

A good way to find a place is to look in the "for rent" ads of the newspaper. Like want ads for employment, they are in the Classified section of the newspaper. Rental ads are organized in different ways. But usually, you will find these groupings:

☐ Apartments for Rent

☐ Roommates Wanted

☐ Houses to Share

Newspapers often list rental apartments by neighborhood as well. Suppose you need an apartment close to your job. First see if there are separate rental listings for that part of town.

### Abbreviations in Rental Ads

In Chapter 7, you learned a number of abbreviations to help you understand want ads. There are special abbreviations to learn for rental ads, too. Here are some examples:

apt.: apartment

ba.: bath

br.: bedroom

**Figure It Out**

*What do you think "1/2 ba." stands for?*

frn: furnished

incl.: included

lg.: large

lndry: laundry

kit.: kitchen

nr. trans.: near transportation

prkng: parking

rm: room

sec. dep.: security deposit

unfrn: unfurnished

util.: utilities

w/w cpt.: wall-to-wall carpeting

yd.: yard

---

## Practice

Do the following on a separate piece of paper.

1. Write this rental ad without abbreviations:

   2 br. apt. unf. lndry, lg. yd. $450 plus util. 555-0003

2. Imagine that you want to rent out a room in your two bedroom apartment. Write a rental ad for a roommate. Use abbreviations to keep the ad under 15 words. Remember that each abbreviation stands for one word.

## Practical English Skill 3: Interview Your Landlord

Once you find an interesting place in the rental ads, you can call the listed number. To save time and energy, prepare an interview guide to use over the phone. Think about a living situation that would be ideal for you. Talk to the person who owns the property, or the **landlord**. Then ask key questions. To write an interview guide, follow these steps:

1. Think about your needs.

2. Use the who, what, where, when, and why words to form questions. Write them down.

3. Make several copies of the guide. Each time you call about an apartment, take notes about it.

4. Write a list of pros and cons to help you decide which apartments you really want to look at.

Here is an example of one person's interview guide:

Apartment:

Phone Number:

Person Called:

1. How big is the apartment?
2. How many bedrooms does it have?
3. How many bathrooms does it have?
4. What kind of neighborhood is it in?
5. What is the building like?
6. How close is it to the 51 bus line?
7. Where is the nearest grocery store?
8. Where is the closest park?

### Practice

Write your own interview guide. Include key things you want to know about an apartment before you take the time to look at it. Do you have a dog? Then you'll have to ask if pets are allowed. Do you need a garage? Or will an open parking space do? Write at least five questions on a separate piece of paper.

## Practical English Skill 4: Apply for an Apartment

Suppose you go to look at an apartment. It seems right for you. But there are three other people there who want it, too. The landlord asks each person to fill out a rental application.

Remember that Chapter 8 pointed out that job applications should be filled out neatly. Rental applications should also be neat. Most of the time, you will need to fill out an application on the spot. Here's how to be prepared:

☐ Bring a sharp pencil and an eraser.

☐ Bring a list of **credit references** and a list of **personal references.** These people should be able to **vouch** for you, or say you pay your bills and will make a good **tenant.**

☐ If you have a driver's license, bring it with you. You may need to write down this number on the rental application.

☐ Read the form carefully. Fill in all the blanks. If something doesn't apply to you, write N/A. It stands for **not applicable.**

## Practice

On this page is a sample rental application. Copy it onto a separate piece of paper and fill it out.

**RENTAL APPLICATION**

Property Address: _____ Apt. # _____
Monthly Rental $ _____ Security Deposit $ _____ Proposed Date of Occupancy _____
Name(s) of Applicant(s) _____
Names of other Occupants: _____
Are any of the above under 18? _____
Pets (Number & Type): _____
Present Address: _____
How long? _____ Reason for leaving: _____
Name & Address of Owner Agent: _____
Last Previous Address: _____
How long? _____ Reason for leaving: _____
Name & Address of Owner Agent: _____
Present Employer: _____ How long? _____
Address: _____ Telephone: _____
Employed as: _____ Salary $ _____ per _____
Present Employer of any other Occupant: _____ How long? _____
Address: _____ Telephone: _____
Employed as: _____ Salary $ _____ per _____
Other Income: $ _____ Source: _____
Credit References: (1) _____
Address: _____ Telephone: _____
(2) _____
Address: _____ Telephone: _____
Automobile License # _____ State of Registry: _____
Make & Model: _____ Year: _____ Color: _____
**IN CASE OF EMERGENCY**
Name of Closest Relative: _____ Relationship: _____
Address: _____ Telephone: _____
**AUTHORIZATION TO VERIFY INFORMATION**
I Authorize Owner/Agent to Verify the above information, including but not limited to obtaining a Credit Report.
Date _____ , 19 _____ Applicant: _____
Telephone: _____
****NOTE:   IF YOU GIVE A DEPOSIT, YOU SHOULD GET A RECEIPT WHICH SPECIFIES WHAT THE DEPOSIT IS FOR. CALIFORNIA CIVIL CODE SECTION 1950.5 COVERS DEPOSITS AND THEIR USES.

**If You Had to Choose**

*Imagine that you are a landlord. Would neatness and good spelling help you choose a tenant? Why?*

## Practical English Skill 5: Sign a Lease

Often, after being approved for an apartment, you will have to sign a **lease**. A lease is a legal contract. It outlines the agreement between you and your landlord.

Leases can be very simple and easy to understand. Or they can be long, written in small print, and full of legal terms. Before you sign a lease, you should read it carefully. You should make notes about anything you do not understand. Then you should get those questions answered. Here are some key pieces of information that should be included in the lease:

**Use Your Note-Taking Skills**

*When you move into an apartment, take notes on anything that is already damaged. Keep one copy and give one copy to your landlord.*

☐ The time period the lease covers. Some leases are month-to-month. Others last for six months to a year. While the lease is in effect, the landlord cannot raise the rent. But you are **obligated** to stay for that whole period. When the lease is up, the landlord can legally ask you to leave. The landlord can also increase your rent, or make other changes in any terms of the lease.

☐ Who pays for **utilities**? Sometimes the landlord pays for gas and electricity. Sometimes landlords just pay for garbage collection and water. Make sure you know exactly what you are paying for.

☐ First and last months' rents. Some landlords want you to pay two months in rent. They do this  in case you leave without notice or do not pay your rent.

You may want to walk through the apartment with the landlord the day you move in. Have the landlord sign the paper with your notes. This will help you get your security deposit back when it is time to leave.

☐ The security deposit. You may have to pay a security deposit. This is an amount of money the landlord keeps if you damage the apartment. If you leave the apartment in good condition, this money is returned to you. This is called a **refundable deposit**.

☐ The cleaning deposit. This fee is usually not refundable. It is used to clean and paint the apartment after you are gone. Make sure you ask your landlord how this deposit is different from a security deposit.

## Practice

**What Does It Mean?**
What do you think people mean when they say, "Read the fine print"?

Write one or two sentences explaining these words or phrases that might be found on a lease. Answer on a separate piece of paper.

1. month-to month

2. $75 cleaning fee

3. first and last months' rents and security deposit due upon moving in

4. landlord pays for all utilities

# Chapter Review

---

## Chapter Summary

- ☐ Use lists of pros and cons to help you compare living situations.

- ☐ Rental ads are a good place to find rentals. Rental ads can be organized by type of living situation and neighborhood. Rental ads usually use abbreviations to describe apartments.

- ☐ Write an interview guide to learn more about apartments over the phone. Then decide if the apartments are worth looking at.

- ☐ Be prepared to fill out rental applications when you look at an apartment. Neatness counts!

- ☐ Read leases carefully, looking for key words and phrases. Know what you are signing.

## Putting Skills Together

How could the library help you learn more about leases?

## Developing Writing Skills

Describe what you think is a perfect apartment. Consider these questions: Do you want to live alone? Do you want to have a fireplace? What kind of furniture do you want? Use a separate piece of paper for your answer.

## Chapter Quiz

Use a separate piece of paper to answer these questions. Write one or two sentences in each answer.

1. How can lists of pros and cons help you find a place to live?

2. What does each of the following abbreviations mean: ba., nr., util., lndry.?

3. How can want ads grouped by neighborhood help you find a place suited for you?

4. What are three questions you might include on a landlord interview guide?

5. How can using an interview guide save you time?

6. What are two things you should bring with you to fill out a rental application?

7. Why is it important to be prepared to fill out a rental application on the spot?

8. What is a lease?

9. What is the difference between a security deposit and a cleaning fee?

10. Suppose a lease is long and hard to read. Should you just trust the landlord and sign it? Explain.

## Vocabulary Review

On a separate piece of paper, write three sentences of your own. Use one or more of these vocabulary words in each sentence:

tenant                    lease                    vouch

# *14* Getting Around

*People use practical English skills to locate and use public transportation schedules. Reading a bus schedule is like reading a chart.*

## Chapter Learning Objectives

- ☐ Use a telephone book to learn about public transportation.
- ☐ Read a bus schedule.
- ☐ Use a street index and map.
- ☐ List three steps in studying for a driver's test.

## Words to Know

**car pool**   group of people who share car rides

**intersection**   the place where two streets cross each other

**points of interest**   interesting things to do and see

**public transportation**   vehicles like buses and subways that are available for anyone to use

**route**   a certain path or direction

It is the morning of Stella's job interview. Her old car breaks down. The last thing she wants to do is cancel this interview. But what can she do?

First she calls her friend Laverne to ask for a ride. But Laverne's roommate says she has already left for work. Then Stella calls the neighborhood gas station. But no one there has time to help her now. A mechanic won't be able to come over and look at her car until noon.

Stella can use some practical English skills to help her through the morning. The first thing she needs to do is to use the telephone book.

## Practical English Skill 1: Find Public Transportation

Your city probably offers some type of **public transportation**. This is transportation that anyone can use. Most kinds of public transportation run with the help of tax dollars. This helps keep the cost of using them low. The most common type of public transportation is the bus. Large cities such as New York City and Washington, D.C., have underground trains or subways. In San Francisco, ferries carry workers across the bay, and cable cars carry them up and down the hills.

How do you find public transportion? Use the telephone book. Begin by looking in the front of the white pages. Under government listings, find a general information number for your city or county. Call this number and ask about public transportation in your area. If you know the name of the transportation system, look in the white pages under that name.

***Words for Getting Around***

*Many cities and counties are starting **car pool** agencies. These agencies try to match cars and riders. Car pools save money and make highways less crowded.*

### Practice

Do the following on a separate piece of paper.

1. Imagine you want to know about buses that run through the north side of your city. Make a list of questions you might ask when you call the bus company.

2. Write a list of pros and cons about using public transportation.

3. You know that the bus system in your city is called Tran-Sit. How would you find it in the phone book?

## Practical English Skill 2:  Read a Bus Schedule

Phil picked up a bus schedule from a counter at the library. Now how does he read it?

**English Tip**
If you ever have trouble understanding a schedule, ask a public transportation worker for help.

Reading a bus schedule is like reading any table or chart. Take a look at the bus schedule on page 166. The top of the bus schedule shows the different stops on the bus **route.** The bus stops in that order. In other words, the first stop is Westlake Drive. The second stop is Oakwood Avenue, and so on.

Each column of times under the street stops tells you what time you can catch the bus. The bus stops at Westlake Drive at 5:51 a.m., 6:08 a.m., 6:42 a.m., and 7:02 a.m.

You need to know the street the bus is traveling on, too. A map of the route is included on a bus schedule so you'll know the correct place on Westlake Drive, Oakwood Avenue, and so on.

Now, suppose you are getting on the bus at Westlake Drive. Your job interview is near the Elm Street stop. You can find out how long it will take you to get to Elm Street by using the rows. Do the following:

**Step 1:** Suppose you are getting on the Westlake Drive stop at 7:02. Put your finger on the row where 7:02 begins.

**Step 2:** Run your finger along that row until it is under the Elm Street stop.

**Step 3:** Your finger should be on 7:38 a.m. Subtract 7:02 from 7:38. You can see that it will take you 36 minutes to get to Elm Street.

| Westlake Dr | Oakwood Ave. | Fruitvale St. | Sunset Blvd. | Elm St. |
|---|---|---|---|---|
| 5:51 | 5:58 | 6:04 | 6:12 | 6:20 |
| 6:08 | 6:16 | 6:25 | 6:37 | 6:48 |
| 6:42 | 6:50 | 6:58 | 7:08 | 7:19 |
| 7:02 | 7:10 | 7:18 | 7:26 | 7:38 |

## Practice

Use a separate piece of paper to answer the following questions. Refer to the bus schedule on this page.

1. You need to be on Elm Street by 7:30. What is the latest time you can get on the bus at Westlake Drive?

2. What stops are between Westlake Drive and Sunset Boulevard?

3. What is the earliest time you can catch a bus on Fruitvale Street?

## Practical English Skill 3: Use a Street Index

Whether you are driving yourself or taking the bus, it is good to know how to use a street index. Street indexes are on maps. You can use a street index to find streets. You can also use it to find interesting things to do and see. On a street index, such things are called **points of interest.**

A street index is like the index of a book. It has several headings under which alphabetical listings are given. Here are some examples:

Parks

Children's Park A-2

Hobie's Park Q-7

Points of Interest

City Hall C-3

City Zoo X-7

Streets

Baker Street C-2

Bush Street E-2

Heart Street B-3

Henry Street C-3

Jones Street A-2

Martin Luther King, Jr., Way A-4

Parker Street B-2

Penny Street A-1

You can see the letters and numbers after each listing. These tell you how to find what you are looking for on a map. Look at the map on page 168.

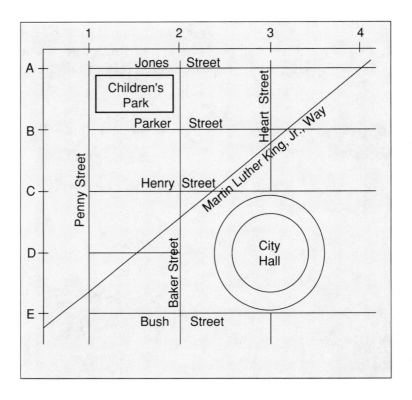

On the left side of the map are letters. Along the top of the map are numbers. Suppose you want to find Martin Luther King, Jr., Way. The street index lists it as A-4. To find this street, put one finger on A. Run it across the map until it is under the number 4. Your finger is at the **intersection** of Martin Luther King, Jr., Way and Jones Street.

Large city maps index hundreds of streets and points of interest. Knowing how to use the index is a good way to get to know your city.

## Practice

Look at the map and index on pages 167 and 168. Then use a separate piece of paper to answer the following questions.

*What are two points of interest in your city or town?*

1. What intersection is at point C-2 on the map?

2. What points of interest are on the map?

3. Explain how you would use the index to find Bush Street.

## Practical English Skill 4: Interpret Road Signs

Now that Maggie is on her own, she has decided to buy a car. She is going to use all the English skills she learned in Units I and II to get a great deal. But does she have the English skills she needs to get a driver's license?

Most people do not connect English skills and driving. But how would you like to be on the road with someone who couldn't read these signs?

*Black and white road signs tell you what to do. You must read them carefully when you are driving.*

Of course, some signs do not have any words. It is the driver's job to know what those signs stand for. Here are some examples:

**Words for Driving**
*Do you know what the word "Yield" means on a sign? If you need help, use a dictionary or ask a friend.*

*This sign tells you there is a light signal ahead.*

*This sign tells you that an intersection is coming up.*

## Practice

On a separate piece of paper, write what you think each of these signs means.

## Practical English Skill 5: Study for Your Driver's Test

*A Listening Test*

*In some states, you can have the driver's test read to you. Do you think this is a good idea? Explain.*

To get a driver's license, you will usually have to take two tests. One is a test of your driving ability. You will have to drive a car with an examiner riding with you, watching what you do. The other is a written, multiple choice test. It asks you about laws and driving procedures. Most state motor vehicle departments have a book you can use to study for this test. Once you get this book, you should

1. Read it in small sections. You will remember more if you study a little each day.

**Brush Up
on the Basics**

*What are key words?
If you need help, turn
back to Chapter 1,
page 5, and read
about key words.*

2. Take notes on what you read. Look for key words.

3. Before you take the test, look back over the suggestions for taking objective tests. You will find them in Chapter 4, on page 49.

4. If you fail the test, ask if you can keep it. Take the test home and study the answers you got wrong. Then take the test again when you are ready.

To apply for a driver's license, you will need to have some identification with you. This will usually be your birth certificate and social security card. How do you find the state Department of Motor Vehicles office nearest you? Look in the state government section of your phone book.

Many states require you to get a learner's permit before you apply for a driver's license. A learner's permit allows you to drive a car only when a licensed driver is seated beside you. You must always carry this permit with you when you are learning to drive.

Once you pass all the tests, you will have to pay a fee to get your driver's license. Remember that a driver's license is a legal document. If you misplace your license, you can get a duplicate at the Department of Motor Vehicles. Your license may also be suspended or taken away for a number of reasons. Reckless driving, speeding, and drunk driving are common reasons for losing a driver's license. If the police suspect that you are driving drunk, they can ask you to take a sobriety test. If you refuse to take the test, your license can be taken away—even if you're not drunk.

## Practice

Answer the following questions on a separate piece of paper.

1. How are English skills and driving connected?
2. What are two common road signs, and what do they mean?
3. Suppose you do not know the driving laws in your state. How can you find out about them?
4. How would you go about studying for a driver's license test?
5. How could you find the Department of Motor Vehicles office nearest you?
6. What can you do if you misplace your driver's license?

# Chapter Review

## Chapter Summary

☐   Information about public transportation can be found in the telephone book. Try city and county governments first for information.

☐   Bus schedules tell you at what times buses leave and arrive at certain stops. Reading a schedule is like reading a chart.

☐   Most maps have street indexes. These indexes list streets, points of interest, and more. Numbers and letters on the map help you find indexed streets.

☐   Driving and English skills go together. Drivers must read signs and give meanings to picture signs. They must also study for a written driver's test.

## Putting Skills Together

On a separate piece of paper, take notes on this paragraph. Remember to write only key words.

*State law says you must never drive faster than is safe for the conditions at the present time. Don't go by the speed limit sign. Weather conditions, the number of cars on the road, and other things can make driving at the posted speed limit dangerous. Under normal conditions, the state highway speed limit is 55 miles per hour.*

Now choose the best answer to this question.

On state highways, you should always drive

   a. the speed limit.

   b. at a speed that suits present conditions.

   c. slowly in heavy traffic.

## Chapter Quiz

Use a separate piece of paper to answer the following questions. Write one or two sentences in each answer.

1. What are two pros and two cons for using public transporation?

2. Imagine you are new in a city. How would you go about finding public transportation?

3. Describe what you will find on a bus schedule.

4. What is a street index?

5. Sam is on vacation. How can a map help him find interesting things to see in the city he is visiting?

6. Draw a small map. Show how the map uses numbers and letters to help a person find streets.

7. What two kinds of tests must a person take to get a driver's license?

8. What is a Department of Motor Vehicles?

9. How are English skills and driving linked?

10. What are three steps in studying for the written license test?

## Vocabulary Review

Match the words on the left to their meanings on the right. Write the numbers and corresponding letters on a separate piece of paper.

1. public transportation       a. interesting things to do and see

2. route                       b. people who share car rides

3. car pool                    c. the place where two roads cross

4. points of interest          d. transportation anyone can use

5. intersection                e. path or direction

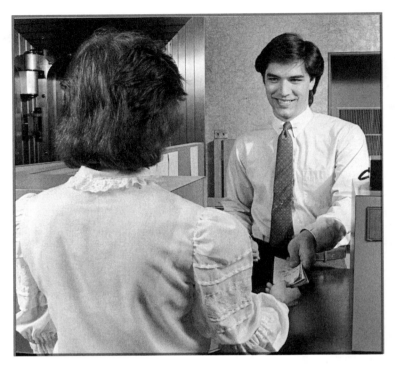

*English skills can help you keep track of your money. Using an interview guide can help you shop for the best checking account.*

## Chapter Learning Objectives

- ☐ Write an interview guide for banking.
- ☐ Write a check.
- ☐ Fill in a check register.
- ☐ List two key words to look for when getting a credit card.
- ☐ List four key items to read on bills.

## Words to Know

**annual fee**   yearly charge

**balance**   amount

**check register**   record book for checks

**deposit**   money that is put in an account; to put money in an account

**interest**   percent earned or charged on money

**minimum**   least

**transaction**   an exchange, usually involving money

One day, Jim got a letter in the mail. It was from his bank. Jim's checks had been bouncing all over town. He owed the bank money. He owed businesses money. Jim did not know what had happened.

Then he stopped to think about it. A couple of times he had needed cash late in the evening. He had used the Automatic Teller Machine (ATM) at his bank to withdraw money. Then he forgot to record those withdrawals in his check register. It simply slipped his mind.

Jim had no idea he had been writing bad checks. If only he had used the English skills in this chapter to manage his money!

## Practical English Skill 1: Write an Interview Guide

An important part of living on your own is having a checking account. Checking accounts can make your life easier. You don't have to carry large amounts of cash around. You can mail checks to pay your bills. You can **deposit** your paycheck in the account and know that the money is safe.

You can open a checking account at a bank, a savings and loan association, or a credit union. Some people think that these organizations are run by the government. They are not. They are businesses just like the store on the corner. They stay in business because you pay them to take care of your money.

*Use Your English Skills*
*How would you find banks to call?*

For this reason, it is a good idea to shop around for a checking account. You can begin by writing an interview guide with the who, what, where, when, and why questions. Here are some key words to help you write the guide:

**Minimum deposit**

Most banks want you to start the account with a certain amount of money. This is called the **minimum** deposit. Find out what the amount is for each bank you interview.

**Check printing fee**

Some banks charge you for printing your checks. Other banks give free checks.

**Brush Up on the Basics**

*Do you remember how to take notes? If you need help, turn to page 5 to review note-taking.*

## Monthly service charges

Banks often charge a monthly fee just to keep your account open. They take this amount out of your account as a service charge. Sometimes they also charge you for each check you write.

## Minimum balance

Sometimes banks want you to keep a certain amount of money in your account. This is called a minimum **balance**. If you go below that amount, they might charge you extra fees. Or they may close your account.

## Interest

Some banks pay you **interest** on your checking account. This means that you earn a certain amount of money based on the amount in your account. Here is an example. Imagine you have $100.00 in your checking account. The bank says it will pay you 6% annual interest on it. This comes to .5% interest each month. At the end of the month, the bank adds fifty cents to your account. You have earned fifty cents in interest in one month.

Use your interview guide with several banks. Take notes, and compare what you find out. Then choose the bank that gives you a good deal and is easy for you to use.

## Practice

Use a separate piece of paper to answer these questions.

1. What would you ask when shopping for a checking account? Write at least five questions.

2. John interviewed two banks. He found that Bank X offers a checking account with no minimum balance required. For this account there is a monthly fee of $5.50, and a 20-cent charge for each check he writes. Bank Y offers an account with no monthly fee and no check charge. But John must keep a minimum balance of $500 in the bank. If he goes below that amount, the bank will charge him $20.00. John has exactly $500. What should he do?

## Practical English Skill 2: Fill Out a Check

Once you get your checking account, you will be sent your own set of checks. Each check will have your name, address, and account number on it.

The amount you are writing the check for, in numbers

The date you write the check

Numbers that identify the bank

The check number. You will write this number down later in your check register.

Your personal information printed on the check

The person or company you are writing the check to

The amount you are writing the check for

Your personal note about the check

Your checking account number

Joe Jones
1162 Lily Drive
Lily, CA 94000

90/7400
3255

256

July 7 19,90

Pay to
the order of   The Corner Market   $ 15.73

Sixteen and 73/100 ———————— Dollars

Bank of Lily
1173 Howe St.
Lily, CA 94000

Your signature

For Groceries          Joe Jones

3210  6789  4216

To write a check, just fill in the blanks. The model at the bottom of page 180 shows you a filled-out check and explains the parts.

## Practice

**Your All-Important Signature**
*Once your check is signed, it can be cashed. Sign it only after all other information is filled in.*

Use a separate piece of paper to answer the following questions.

1. Where is the account number of Joe Jones's check?
2. What kinds of personal information are printed on the check?
3. Where can you find the check number?
4. On a separate piece of paper, draw a blank check. Fill it in. Pay $20.00 (twenty dollars) to a friend. Make a personal note that you are paying back a loan.

## Practical English Skill 3: Use a Check Register

Once you write a check, you should record it in your **check register**. This is a record that comes with your checkbook. The check register is like a chart or table. You simply look at the heading of each column. Then you fill in the information. Here is an example:

| Check Number | Date | Transaction | (-) Payment | (-) Fee (if any) | (+) Deposit | Balance |
|---|---|---|---|---|---|---|

**What Would Happen?**

*What could happen if you didn't use your check register?*

You can learn a few things from Joe Jones's check register. The word **transaction** refers to what took place. Notice that Joe Jones did not write in a fee. This is because he is not charged by his bank for writing checks. If Joe deposits money, he will record the amount in the register as well.

## Practice

Imagine that Joe deposits $90.00 into his account on May 15, 1991. On a separate piece of paper, show what his check register would look like.

## Practical English Skill 4: Know Key Words for Credit Cards

The time will come when you get an offer in the mail. It will read something like this:

*We're saving a credit card with your name on it! Just fill in the application and send it back to us. Charge up to $1500 on your new Best Credit Card.*

It sounds great. Buy now, pay later. But before you sign up for a credit card, put some of your English skills to work. Here are some key words to look for when you are considering using a credit card:

☐ Annual fee

Credit card companies, like banks, make money when you use their services. Most credit cards charge you an **annual fee**. This is a yearly charge that you must pay the company. It is often between $10 and $30 per year.

☐ Interest

The company makes most of its money by charging you interest. Here is how credit card interest works.

You buy a suit for $200 using your credit card. When the bill comes, you don't have the money to pay it. "I'll wait until next month," you say to yourself.

The next month, your bill is $203.00. The credit card company charged you 18% annual interest on the $200.00. This comes to 1-1/2% interest per month. Now you owe even more. And if you didn't make any payment last month, you will probably have to pay an extra $5.00 for a late fee.

**Think English**
*Letters from credit card companies are often very long. You have to read carefully to find information on fees and interest. Do you think the credit card companies do this on purpose?*

Credit cards are good things to have. They come in handy during emergencies. But when you apply for one, you should know exactly what you are getting into. Read the small print on letters that invite you to get credit cards. Read applications carefully. Find out what the annual fee and annual interest are. And each time you use the card, remember that a bill is coming at the end of the month!

## Practice

Use a separate piece of paper to answer the following questions.

1. What is a credit card?

2. Gloria gets a letter inviting her to apply for a credit card. What two key pieces of information should she look for in the letter?

3. What are two pros and two cons for using credit cards?

## Practical English Skill 5: Read Bills

When you are living on your own, that credit card bill is not the only bill you will get. You will get phone bills, electricity bills, and gas bills. If you own a home, you will get tax bills. Bills are not pleasant. But they are a fact of life.

When you get a bill, use your English skills to read it carefully. Sometimes companies make mistakes when they prepare your bill. It is up to you to make sure the bills are correct. And, if they are not, it is up to you to get them corrected.

Here are some key words to look for when you read a bill:

☐ Total amount due or balance

This is the amount of money you owe the company.

☐ Explanation of charges

Companies break down the amount on a bill to show exactly what you've been charged for. The telephone company, for example, will list each of your calls. The gas company will show you how much energy you used. A credit card company will list each item you charged. Read these items carefully. It is the only way to know whether you are being charged the right amount.

☐ Previous balance

This shows the amount you owed before this new bill. If it has not been paid, it will be added to your current charges.

☐ Payments made

Here the business shows how much you have paid on your account since you were last billed. Look to see that this amount has been deducted from your previous balance.

☐ Taxes, interest, service fees

These are extra charges added to your bill.

☐ Due date

Somewhere on the bill is a due date. If you do not pay the bill by that date, you may be charged extra.

☐ Account number

This is the number a business uses to keep track of each customer. If you have a question about your bill, this is the number you use to identify yourself.

Bills will often list a phone number you can call if you have questions about charges. Don't hesitate to use it! Have your account number, questions, and note pad ready when you call.

No two bills are alike. You must study each bill carefully to find the information you are looking for. But it is well worth the trouble.

## Practice

Study this phone bill. Then answer the questions below.

| | Account Number | | 000-000-1111 | | | | Page 1 | |
|---|---|---|---|---|---|---|---|---|
| | Statement Date | | Oct. 5, 1991 | | | | | |

| Account | Previous bill | | | | 18.34 | | |
|---|---|---|---|---|---|---|---|
| Summary | Payments applied through Sept. 7, 1991 | | | | 18.34CR | | |
| | Balance   *** Thank You for Your Payment *** | | | | | .00 | |
| | Current charges: | | | | | | |
| | Pacific Bell (Page 2) | | | | | | |
| | CURRENT CHARGES DUE BY Nov. 5, 1991 | | | | | 9.08 | |
| **Total Due** | | | | | | 9.08 | |

| | Itm | Date | Time | Min * | Place and Number Called | | | Charge |
|---|---|---|---|---|---|---|---|---|
| Calls | 1 | Sep 8 | 957A | 4 DD | BERKELEY | CA | 415 555 6903 | .97 |
| | 2 | Sep 21 | 932A | 4 DD | BERKELEY | CA | 415 555 6903 | .97 |
| | 3 | Sep23 | 918A | 1 DD | BERKELEY | CA | 415 555 6902 | .31 |
| | 4 | Sep23 | 438P | 5 DD | BERKELEY | CA | 415 555 6902 | 1.19 |
| | 5 | Sep29 | 1137A | 1 DD | SAN FRAN | CA | 415 555 9476 | .34 |
| | * | See Rate Key on Reverse | | | | | | |
| | | | | | Subtotal | | | $3.78 |

| | Itm | | | | | Charge |
|---|---|---|---|---|---|---|
| Monthly | 12 | Basic Monthly Service Charge | | | | $4.75 |
| Charges | 13 | Tax:      Fed:     .47      911: | | | .08 | .55 |
| | | Monthly Charges | | Subtotal | | $5.30 |

| Total | | Current Charges | | | | $9.08 |
|---|---|---|---|---|---|---|

1. What does this person owe?

2. How much of the total bill is for phone calls?

3. How much of the total bill is for monthly charges?

4. How much does the person pay in federal taxes?

5. How much does the person pay for the 911 service tax?

6. How much was the person's bill the previous month?

7. When is the current bill due?

8. The person was out of town on September 23. No one was staying at his house. Does he have a reason to call the phone company? Explain.

Telephone costs can add up quickly. Calls from a pay phone usually cost more than calls from a home or business phone. For example, compare these weekday rates for a 3-minute call from San Francisco, California, to some other cities. (All rates and charges shown may have changed since this book was written.)

| Unassisted 3-Minute Call | | | |
| --- | --- | --- | --- |
| From San Francisco to: | Distance | Home Phone Rate | Pay Phone Rate |
| Hayward | 30 miles | $ .45 | $ .60 |
| Santa Rosa | 60 miles | .55 | .75 |
| New York City | 3,000 miles | 1.32 | 2.95 |

## Practice

Use the table to answer these questions. Write your answers on a separate sheet of paper.

1. How much more would it cost to call Hayward on a pay phone than on a home phone?

2. How much more would it cost to call Santa Rosa?

3. How much more would it cost to call New York?

# Chapter Review

## Chapter Summary

- ☐ English skills can help you keep track of your money.

- ☐ Use an interview guide to shop for the best checking account.

- ☐ Fill out checks completely and carefully. Sign your name to the check only after it is filled out.

- ☐ Fill out the check register as you would any chart. It will help you keep track of how much money is in your account.

- ☐ Look for the annual fee and interest when applying for a credit card.

- ☐ Read bills carefully to make sure you are being charged the right amount.

## Putting Skills Together

Imagine that you have shopped for checking accounts. You found a good deal. The bank is at the corner of Main and Harrison.

You are new in town and don't know the streets. What English skills could you use to find the bank?

## Developing Writing Skills

Do you think credit cards should be done away with? Write your answer on a separate piece of paper. Include a topic sentence, at least two supporting sentences, and a closing sentence.

## Chapter Quiz

Use a separate piece of paper to answer the following questions. Write one or two sentences in each answer.

1. What are two good reasons to have a checking account?
2. What are three questions you might put on your interview guide for checking accounts?
3. What are two fees a bank might charge?
4. What does *minimum balance* mean?
5. What are the seven column headings on a check register?
6. What is an annual service fee for a credit card?
7. Why should you read the small print on a credit card application?
8. Why should you read your bills carefully?
9. Suppose you have a question about your bill. How do you know where to call?
10. How do you know when to pay your bill?

## Vocabulary Review

Match the words on the left to their meanings on the right. Write the numbers and corresponding letters on a separate piece of paper.

1. deposit         a. yearly charge
2. minimum         b. an exchange, usually involving money
3. transaction     c. amount
4. balance         d. least
5. annual fee      e. money that is put in an account; to put money in an account
6. interest        f. percent earned or charged on money

# Unit Review

1. Explain the difference between a credit reference and a personal reference.

2. Explain why a landlord often asks for two month's rent in advance.

3. What would a sloppy, incomplete rental application say about you to the landlord?

4. Newspaper rental ads are organized in three groups. Name the three groups.

5. Suppose you are an ad writer for the County Transportation District. Write three good reasons why people should take the bus instead of driving.

6. Who can issue you a driver's license—the federal government, the state, or the city?

7. Name two ways that a street index is like the index of a book.

8. A bus schedule shows the different stops along a bus route. What else does it show?

9. What happens if your bank account falls below the minimum balance?

10. How does a credit card company earn most of its money—by charging interest or by charging annual fees?

11. Is a bank a business or a government institution?

12. You see the words "due date" on a bill. What do these words mean?

# Unit Five

# English for Citizens

**Chapter 16**

Working with the
Government

**Chapter 17**

Paying Taxes

# Chapter *16* Working with the Government

*English skills help you work with the government. Whether you're applying for a driver's license or studying election issues, you will need to understand what you read.*

## Chapter Learning Objectives

☐ Locate key government agencies in the phone book.

☐ Fill out government forms.

☐ List pros, cons, and examples of bias in campaign materials.

## Words to Know

**ballot**   a list of people running for office; also a list of local laws that must be voted on

**bias**   an attitude that is strongly or unfairly on one side of an issue

**birth certificate**   official record containing a person's family and birth information

**editorial**   a statement of opinion

**election**   choosing of government leaders or local laws by vote

**military**   having to do with the army, navy, or other defense group

**proposition**   a local or state law, or measure, that must be voted on

**register**   to sign up

**The Government in Your Life**
*Have you ever had dealings with a government agency? When?*

The government controls more of your life than you might think. Public schools, for example, are part of local and state governments. The state government has the power to give and take away your driver's license. You must let the government know when you want to get married. And you must pay taxes to the government in order to fund these and other services.

You can use English skills to work with the government. These skills can also help you have some say in how government services are run.

## Practical English Skill 1: Use the Telephone Book

Mitzi is applying for a driver's license. She has waited in a long line. The clerk looks at her and says, "Did you bring proof of your age?" Mitzi has brought her mother, who tells the clerk how old Mitzi is. The clerk tells Mitzi that he needs more proof.

A driver's license or state identification card can be used as proof of age. But to get either one of these things, you will need your **birth certificate**. The birth certificate is an official county government record of when you were born. It also contains family and health information about you. How do you get one?

*For Your Information*
*Are you planning to leave the country? You might need a passport. Contact your local postal service for information on how to apply.*

To get information from any government agency, start with the telephone book. Most white pages begin with an *Easy Reference List*. This list contains the most-often-used government telephone numbers. Look up the heading Birth Certificates or Birth Records. You will probably find the number you need.

What if an agency is not in the Easy Reference List? Ask yourself if the agency is run by the city, county, state, or federal government. Birth certificates are kept by the county in which you were born. So you would need to look under the county government listings.

What if you were born far away from where you are now living? Then you may want to write for information on how to obtain your birth certificate.

**Brush Up on The Basics**

*Do you remember how to write a business letter? If you need help, turn to pages 104-105 to review the business letter form.*

Suppose you do not know which government–city, county, state, or federal–runs the agency you are looking for. You do not even know the name of the agency. Scan the listings under all the government agencies. If there is an information number, call it. And if you get the wrong agency, tell the person who answers the phone what you want. That person may be able to tell you the right number to call.

### Practice

1. Suppose you want to find the nearest state Department of Motor Vehicles.

   a. Where is the first place you would look?

   b. Where is the second place you would look?

2. The following list is from the Easy Reference List of a telephone book. Scan the list and find the number for

   a. dog licenses in Richmond

   b. marriage licenses

   c. bicycle licenses in Frankville

### LICENSES–PERMITS–REGISTRATIONS
**Auto and Boat Registrations–Plates–Permits**

| | |
|---|---|
| Frankville | 555-0098 |
| Oakville | 555-1123 |
| Richmond | 555-1120 |
| Birth and Death | 555-0066 |

**Business**

| | |
|---|---|
| Richmond | 555-1110 |
| Frankville | 555-7777 |
| Oakville | 555-0276 |
| Salem | 555-8898 |

**Bicycle**

| | |
|---|---|
| Richmond | 555-3342 |
| Frankville | 555-3456 |
| Oakville | 555-7693 |

**Dog**

| | |
|---|---|
| Richmond | 555-8664 |
| Oakville | 555-7694 |
| **Marriage** | 555-9999 |

## Practical English Skill 2: Fill Out Forms

To apply for any kind of license, you'll need to fill out a form. The government wants those forms filled out completely. An incomplete form might mean you would have to go back to the end of the line.

Whenever you have to fill out a government form, do these things:

1. Read over the form carefully. If you don't understand a word or a direction, use a dictionary. If you still don't understand, ask a government worker what it means.

**How Does It Feel?**

*Have you ever been told to go back to the end of the line because you did not fill out a form correctly?*

2. Fill out the form completely. Print in neat letters.

3. Some forms ask for a signature. Sign your name and write the date.

Filling out forms correctly and completely the first time will save you time and energy.

## Practice

**Part 1.** In order to vote in a government **election**, you must first **register**. Refer to the boxed information below to answer these questions. This information is found on the front of a State of California Voter Registration Card.

# REGISTER TO VOTE
## VOTER INFORMATION

1. You must be a citizen of the United States.

2. You must be a resident of California.

3. You must be 18 years of age or older as of the day of the next election to vote.

4. You must NOT be in prison or on parole for the conviction of a felony.

5. In order to vote in any specific election you must be registered 29 days prior to that election. If your affidavit is complete, your registration is effective upon receipt by the county clerk; however, you should not consider yourself registered until you receive a Voter Notification Card. If you do NOT receive a Voter Notification Card call the county clerk.

6. If you wish to receive an absentee ballot by mail, a written application must be on file with the county clerk's office at least 7 days before the election. Thereafter you may apply for and vote an absentee ballot at that office either in person or through an authorized representative.

7. For election information call the number listed below:

Telephone: (707) 555-6201

1. Do you have to be 18 years old to register to vote? Explain.

2. How many days **before** an election must you register?

3. Suppose you need information about the election. What number might you call?

| 1 | Name | first | middle | last | | I am a citizen of the United States and will be at least 18 years of age at the time of the next election. I am not imprisoned or on parole for the conviction of a felony. I certify under penalty of perjury under the laws of the State of California, that the information on this affidavit is true and correct. | | |
|---|---|---|---|---|---|---|---|---|
| 2 | Residence | no. | street | apt. no. | | | | |
| | City | County | | Zip Code | **11** Signature | | | Date |
| 3 | Describe location of residence (cross streets) | | | | **WARNING** Perjury is punishable by imprisonment in State prison for two, three or four years. §126 Penal Code. | | | |
| 4 | Mailing Address (if different) | | | | **12** Signature of person assisting (if any) | | | |
| | City | State | | Zip Code | **13** **PRIOR REGISTRATION** If you are now or have ever been registered to vote, show your latest known registraton below. | | | |
| 5 | Date of Birth  mo.    day    year | | **8** Occupation | | Name | | | |
| 6 | Birthplace  Name of U.S. State of Foreign country | | | | Former Address | | | |
| 7 | Political Party (Check One) | | **9** Telephone (Optional) | | City      County      State | | | |
| | ☐ American Independent Party | | **10** I prefer election materials in: (Check one) | | | | | |
| | ☐ Democratic Party | | | | | | | |
| | ☐ Libertarian Party | | | | Political Party | | | |
| | ☐ Peace and Freedom Party | | ☐ English | | | | | |
| | ☐ Republican Party | | ☐ Español | | OFFICE USE | | | |
| | ☐ Decline to State | | ☐ Chinese | | | | | |
| | ☐ Other _____ (Specify) | | | | | | | |

**Part 2:** Study the sample voter registration form.

Refer to it to answer these questions.

1. Read the form. Make a list of words or directions you do not understand. Use the dictionary to help you find word meanings.
2. On a separate piece of paper, write all the information you would have to include on the form. Print neatly.

## Practical English Skill 3: Decide How to Vote

*Did You Know?*

*If you are a male between 18 and 25 years old, you must register with the Selective Service System. The federal government uses this list in case of war or other **military** emergency. Those persons who are registered can be called into service.*

Voting wisely is an important way of working with government. It is a way of being heard. It is a way of taking control.

In most elections, you will be choosing from among several people who are running for different offices. You may also be choosing to vote for or against new state or local laws and taxes. Sometimes these items are called measures or **propositions.** All these choices are listed on a **ballot.**

Before you cast your vote, you must become informed about the people and issues you will be voting for. Here are some ways to prepare:

☐ Read voter pamphlets published by the government. These pamphlets present both sides to issues or laws. They do not tell you how to vote.

☐ Listen to **editorials** on TV, or read editorials in the newspaper. Also read campaign material put out by committees and parties. But remember, this kind of material is **biased.** It gives one person's or one group's opinion, and it is meant to get your vote. It rarely tells both sides of an issue fairly.

☐ As you read campaign material, take notes. List pros and cons. Then make your decision.

*English for Citizenship*

*If you are not a citizen, you will have to become one before you can vote. The Department of Naturalization will tell you what steps you must take in order to become a citizen.*

## Practice

Here is an editorial printed in a local paper. Read it, and then answer the questions on page 201.

### On Measure A

If passed, Measure A would require all businesses in the city to pay a child-care tax. This tax would help run child-care centers in the area. It sounds like a good cause. But think about it.

How will businesses pay for this tax? They will raise prices. And new businesses will be less likely to move to our fair city because of this extra tax. This will cost citizens of the city jobs.

The tax is unfair. Let parents pay for their own child care, and let businesses do what they were meant to do. I hope other citizens will join me in voting against Measure A.

*A Concerned Business Owner*

1. What is Measure A?

2. Does this editorial present both sides of the issue? Explain.

3. List any pros or cons you can get from the editorial.

4. Where might you find more information on Measure A?

States have the right to set qualifications for voters, but they may not discriminate because of race, sex, or age. When the United States was first founded, only free, white males were allowed to vote. Now every citizen has that right.

Through the years three amendments were added to the Constitution to guarantee the right to vote. The Fifteenth Amendment, passed in 1870, outlawed discrimination on the basis of race or color. The Nineteenth Amendment, passed in 1920, gave women the right to vote in all elections. The Twenty-sixth Amendment, passed in 1971, gave the vote to all persons 18 or over.

# Chapter Review

## Chapter Summary

☐ The government is a part of your everyday life. English skills can help you work smoothly with the government. They can also help you vote and take part in the government.

☐ Use the telephone book to find government agencies. First, look in the Easy Reference List. Then look under the branch of government that runs the agency. Call the government information number for help. Finally, scan the listings for other agencies that can possibly help you.

☐ Fill out forms neatly and completely to save time. If you do not understand something on a form, ask a government worker what it means.

☐ Read about election issues before you vote. Check to see whether what you are reading or listening to is fair. Take notes, list pros and cons, and then decide on your position.

## Putting Skills Together

Suppose you are not a citizen of the United States. But you want to become one. How would you use the telephone book to find out how to become a citizen? How would you use the library to study for any tests you might have to take?

## Developing Writing Skills

Imagine that in the next election, you will have to vote for or against Measure 31. Measure 31 will ban smoking in all the restaurants in your city. On a separate piece of paper, write at least two pros and two cons for Measure 31. Decide how you will vote. Then write an editorial to the local newspaper in which you give your opinion. Be sure to include the reasons for your opinion.

## Chapter Quiz

Use a separate piece of paper to answer these questions. Write one or two sentences in each answer.

1. What are three times in your life you might need to work with a government agency?

2. What are the four branches of government listed in the phone book?

3. You want to complain about the garbage pickup service in your city. How do you find the number in your telephone book?

4. A form you are filling out uses the word "affidavit." What are two ways you could find out that word's meaning?

5. Why is it a good idea to fill out forms carefully and neatly?

6. What government agency would you go to for a passport application?

7. What are two resources for reading about elections?

8. Suppose you have some election material. At the bottom of the material is this sentence: "Put out by the Committee to Pass Measure 6." Do you think this material tells the whole story? Explain.

9. What should you do as you read election materials?

10. Suppose you have a question about where to vote. How could you use the telephone book to help you?

## Vocabulary Review

On a separate piece of paper, write three sentences of your own. Use at least one of the following vocabulary words in each sentence:

election                    propositions                    bias

*Tax laws and instructions change quite often. Practical English skills help you cope with those changes.*

## Chapter Learning Objectives

☐ Find and list key tax information on W-2 and 1099 forms.

☐ Interpret tax instructions.

☐ Find information in a tax table.

☐ List resources for tax help.

## Words to Know

**dependent**   a person who is supported by another

**extension**   a longer period of time to file taxes

**income tax**   money paid to the government, based on the amount of money made during the year

**itemize**   to list, as deductions

**tax deductions**   costs that can be subtracted from yearly income to help lower taxable income (such as health care costs)

**taxable income**   income that is taxed by the government

**withheld**   held back

**Words for Taxpayers**
*A **dependent** is a person who depends on you for support. Are you a dependent? Or do you have dependents?*

It's almost April 15, the deadline for paying **income tax.** Frank has dozens of forms and instruction booklets. He also has a headache. He doesn't know where to start.

Frank can use English skills to get those taxes done. Many of the skills he will need have already been discussed in this book.

### A Word About Taxes and Skills

Tax laws can change from year to year. When they do, tax forms and tax instructions also change. As you make more money, you will be using different tax forms. This chapter is not meant as tax advice. It will, however, help you practice skills that you can use year after year when you do your taxes—no matter how the laws and your income change.

## Practical English Skill 1: Organize Tax Papers

After January 1, anyone who has been earning money will start getting important tax information in the mail. The most important information is the W-2 form or forms. You will get a W-2 form from the employer or employers you worked for in the previous year.

Below is a sample of a W-2 form. It tells what one person made during the year. This amount is called *Wages, tips, and other compensation.* The W-2 form also tells the taxes that were **withheld** from the person's pay during the year. Notice that each box on the W-2 form has a small number in the left corner. These numbers will be useful for filling out tax forms.

| 1 Control number | | OMB No. 1545-0008 | | | |
|---|---|---|---|---|---|
| 2 Employer's name, address, and ZIP code<br><br>Freeman's Medical Supplies<br>1523 86th Street<br>Dixon, CA 95620 | | | 3 Employer's identification number | | 4 Employer's state I.D. number |
| | | | 5 Statutory employee ☐  Deceased ☐  Pension plan ☐  Legal rep. ☐ | 942 emp. ☐  Subtotal ☐  Deferred compensation ☐  Void ☐ | |
| | | | 6 Allocated tips | | 7 Advance EIC payment |
| 8 Employee's social security number<br>999-00-3534 | 9 Federal income tax withheld<br>$336.70 | | 10 Wages, tips, other compensation<br>$2,900.00 | | 11 Social security tax withheld<br>$207.38 |
| 12 Employee's name, address, and ZIP code<br><br>Maria Ramirez<br>3123 Rosedale Road<br>Dixon, CA 95620 | | | 13 Social security wages<br>$2,900.00 | | 14 Social security tips |
| | | | 16 | | 16a Fringe benefits incl. in Box 10 |
| | | | 17 State income tax<br>$78.06 | 18 State wages, tips, etc. | 19 Name of state |
| | | | 20 Local income tax | 21 Local wages, tips, etc. | 22 Name of locality |

Form **W-2 Wage and Tax Statement**   **1989**
This information is being furnished to the Internal Revenue Service.     **Copy B To be filed with employee's FEDERAL tax return**     Dept. of the Treasury—IRS

Another important tax form is the 1099. This form lists any taxable interest a person received during the year. For example, interest on savings accounts is considered part of **taxable income**. It must be reported to the Internal Revenue Service (IRS). There is a sample 1099 INT form below.

| | | | |
|---|---|---|---|
| 9292 | ☐ VOID  ☐ CORRECTED | For Official Use Only | |

| Type or machine print PAYER'S name, street address, city, state, and ZIP code | Payer's RTN (optional) | OMB No. 1545-0112 | |
|---|---|---|---|
| Dixon County Bank<br>408 Main Street<br>Dixon, CA 95620 | | 1989<br>Statement for<br>Recipients of | **Interest Income** |

| PAYER'S Federal identification number | RECIPIENT'S identification number | 1 Earnings from savings and loan associations, credit unions, bank deposits, bearer certificates of deposit, etc. | | Copy A |
|---|---|---|---|---|
| 11-0225611 | 999-00-3534 | $ 193.42 | | **For Internal Revenue Service Center** |
| Type or machine print RECIPIENT'S name (first, middle, last)<br>Maria Ramirez | | 2 Early withdrawal penalty<br>$ | 3 U.S. Savings Bonds, etc.<br>$ | For Paperwork Reduction Act Notice and instructions for completing this form, see |
| Street address<br>3123 Rosedale Road | | 4 Federal income tax withheld<br>$ | | Instructions for Forms 1099, |
| City, state, and ZIP code<br>Dixon, CA 95620 | | 5 Foreign tax paid (if eligible for foreign tax credit) | 6 Foreign country or U.S. possession | 1098, 5498, 1096, and W-2G. |
| Account number (optional) | | $ | | |

Form **1099-INT**   　　　　　　**Do NOT Cut or Separate Forms on This Page**　　　Department of the Treasury - Internal Revenue Service

As you get tax statements, it is up to you to organize them. Here is an example of how you might go about it.

1. Place all the W-2 forms in one envelope or file folder. Label it "W-2."

2. Place all your 1099 forms showing interest in another envelope or file folder. Label it "Interest."

3. If tax forms and instructions come in the mail, place them in a separate envelope or file folder. Label it "Forms and Instructions."

4. File all papers in a safe place.

Do this for all tax statements you receive, and you will have a good start on getting your taxes done.

## Practice

Use a separate piece of paper to answer these questions.

1. What information is found in Box 10 of the W-2 form on page 206?

2. How much in state taxes was withheld from Maria Ramirez's paycheck in 1989?

3. How much in federal taxes was withheld from Maria Ramirez's paycheck in 1989?

4. Look at Box 1 of the 1099 form on page 207. How much interest did Ms. Ramirez earn in 1989?

5. Suppose you are setting up files for your taxes. What three files are you likely to have?

## Practical English Skill 2: Complete Tax Forms

Tax forms are worksheets. They help you figure out how much tax you owe. They come with step-by-step instructions. A sample of the 1992 1040EZ tax form is on page 209. It is the simplest form you can fill out.

The 1040EZ form is not for everyone. But whether you use it or another kind of tax form, you use the same skills. You read the form. You fill it out carefully and neatly. If you do not understand something, make a note about it. Later, you will get some tips on how to get those questions answered.

Department of the Treasury—Internal Revenue Service

**Form**
# 1040EZ

**Income Tax Return for**
## Single Filers With No Dependents   **1992**

OMB No. 1545-0675

**Name & address**

Use the IRS label (see page 10). If you don't have one, please print.

L A B E L   H E R E

Print your name (first, initial, last)

Home address (number and street). If you have a P.O. box, see page 10.    Apt. no.

City, town or post office, state, and ZIP code. If you have a foreign address, see page 10.

Please print your numbers like this:

$9\ 8\ 7\ 6\ 5\ 4\ 3\ 2\ 1\ 0$

Your social security number

**Please see instructions on the back. Also, see the Form 1040EZ booklet.**

Presidential Election Campaign (See page 10.)
Do you want $1 to go to this fund?

Note: Checking "Yes" will not change your tax or reduce your refund. ▶

Yes   No

Dollars      Cents

**Report your income**

Attach Copy B of Form(s) W-2 here. Attach tax payment on top of Form(s) W-2.

Note: *You must check Yes or No.*

1  Total wages, salaries, and tips. This should be shown in box 10 of your W-2 form(s). Attach your W-2 form(s).    1

2  Taxable interest income of $400 or less. If the total is more than $400, you cannot use Form 1040EZ.    2

3  Add lines 1 and 2. This is your **adjusted gross income.**    3

4  Can your parents (or someone else) claim you on their return?
   ☐ Yes. Do worksheet on back; enter amount from line E here.
   ☐ No. Enter 5,900.00. This is the total of your standard deduction and personal exemption.    4

5  Subtract line 4 from line 3. If line 4 is larger than line 3, enter 0. This is your **taxable income.**    5

**Figure your tax**

6  Enter your Federal income tax withheld from box 9 of your W-2 form(s).    6

7  **Tax.** Look at line 5 above. Use the amount on **line 5** to find your tax in the tax table on pages 22-24 of the booklet. Then, enter the tax from the table on this line.    7

**Refund or amount you owe**

8  If line 6 is larger than line 7, subtract line 7 from line 6. This is your **refund.**    8

9  If line 7 is larger than line 6, subtract line 6 from line 7. This is the **amount you owe.** Attach your payment for full amount payable to the "Internal Revenue Service." Write your name, address, social security number, daytime phone number, and "1992 Form 1040EZ" on it.    9

**Sign your return**

Keep a copy of this form for your records.

I have read this return. Under penalties of perjury, I declare that to the best of my knowledge and belief, the return is true, correct, and complete.

Your signature

X

Date

Your occupation

For IRS Use Only — Please do not write in boxes below.

For Privacy Act and Paperwork Reduction Act Notice, see page 4 in the booklet.   Cat. No. 11329W   Form 1040EZ (1992)

---

## Practice

Refer to the 1040EZ form on page 209 to answer these questions. Use a separate piece of paper.

1. Suppose you do not have an IRS label with your name and address. What should you do?
2. Do you need your social security number to fill out the 1040EZ form?
3. What can you find on the back of the 1040EZ form?
4. Does giving $1 to the Presidential Election Campaign Fund lower your taxes?
5. What two steps on the form help you figure your tax? (Hint: Look at the left column on the form.)

## Practical English Skill 3: Read Tax Instructions

**English for Meaning**
*Take the time to think about what you are reading while you read it. This will help you to learn and remember.*

Tax instructions are not just the step-by-step instructions on the front of the form. The 1040EZ form has instructions on the back as well. For example, suppose you want to know more about the Presidential Election Campaign Fund. Scan the back of the 1040EZ. You will find the heading *Presidential Election Campaign Fund* and this explanation:

*Congress set up this fund to help pay for Presidential election costs. If you want $1 of your tax to go to this fund, check the "Yes" box. If you check "Yes," your tax or refund will not change.*

**Use Your Skills**

*Use your English skills to file a state income tax return, too.*

The 1040EZ and other tax forms come with a tax instruction booklet, too. These booklets can be very helpful. For example, they can help you figure out if you are using the correct form. They can tell you where to call if you have a problem. But to make sense of instructions, you must be skilled in *reading comprehension*. This means that you understand what you read. Here is a good way to practice reading comprehension:

1. If you are reading a paragraph, read it one sentence at a time.

2. Read the first sentence slowly to yourself.

3. Ask yourself, "What did I just read" or "What does this mean I have to do"?

4. If you did not understand the sentence, or do not remember what you just read, read it again.

5. When you understand the sentence, go on.

## Practice

Practice your reading comprehension. Read the instructions in the box on the next page. They refer to the 1040EZ form. Then answer the questions.

**Completing Your Return**

Please print your numbers inside the boxes. Do not type your numbers. Do not use dollar signs. You may round off cents to whole dollars. To do so, drop amounts under 50 cents and increase amounts that are 50 cents or more. For example, $129.49 becomes $129 and $129.50 becomes $130. If you round off, do so for all amounts. But if you have to add two or more amounts to figure the amount to enter on a line, include cents when adding and round off only the total.

1. Should you type numbers on your form?

2. Do you have to round off amounts?

3. How would you round off the amount $245.50?

4. How would you round off the amount $998.45?

5. Can you round off some amounts and not others?

6. You have interest from two accounts. One account earned $26.48 in interest. The other earned $31.19 in interest. Line 2 of the 1040EZ form asks you to enter the amount of your taxable interest income.

   If you are rounding off all your amounts, which of the following is the correct way to figure your interest?

   a. Round off both figures, then add them.

   b. Add them, and then round off the total.

## Practical English Skill 4: Use a Tax Table

Suppose you are filling out form 1040EZ. Line 9 tells you to find the tax on the amount you entered on line 7. It tells you to use a tax table in the tax booklet.

Whenever you are doing your own taxes, you will have to use a tax table. Here is a small sample from a 1992 tax table.

| If 1040A, line 19, OR 1040EZ, line 7 is— | | And you are— | | | |
|---|---|---|---|---|---|
| At least | But less than | Single (and 1040EZ filers) | Married filing jointly * | Married filing sepa- rately | Head of a house- hold |
| | | **Your tax is—** | | | |
| 2,700 | 2,725 | 407 | 407 | 407 | 407 |
| 2,725 | 2,750 | 411 | 411 | 411 | 411 |
| 2,750 | 2,775 | 414 | 414 | 414 | 414 |
| 2,775 | 2,800 | 418 | 418 | 418 | 418 |

Line 7
$2,762
is in this
range.

This column
is for 1040EZ
filers.

You use this tax table just as you would any other table. First, you get the amount of your taxable income from your tax form. Your tax form tells you how to do this. But for now, imagine you have filled out the 1040EZ. Your taxable income is $2,762.

Next, you look at the tax table. You locate the range that your taxable income is in. See the first two columns of the tax table on page 213.

Now, run your finger from the range across to the column under the "Single (and 1040EZ filers)" heading. You can see that the amount of tax you owe is $414.

Read tax tables carefully. Take your time. Always double-check your figures.

## Practice

Use the tax table on page 213. Find the answers to the following questions. Write them on a separate piece of paper.

1. Suppose your taxable income is $2,700. You are married and filing jointly. How much tax do you owe?

2. Suppose your taxable income is $2,780. You are filing as head of household. How much tax do you owe?

## Practical English Skill 5: Get Help When Needed

Suppose you have used all your skills, and you still cannot figure out your taxes. You are not alone. Thousands of people have questions about their tax forms each year. Here are some tips on getting help:

**Brush Up
on the Basics**

*Do you remember
how to use a table of
contents and an
index? If you need
help, turn to pages
18–19 for review.*

1. Your tax booklet has a table of contents and an index. Use them to help you find answers to your questions.

2. Your tax booklet tells you how to locate a toll-free number to the IRS. It also tells you what to do before you call.

3. Libraries often offer free tax help at tax time. Call your library for more information.

4. Private businesses will do your taxes for a fee. To find them, look under Tax Preparation in the yellow pages.

## Practice

Suppose you look in the table of contents of your tax booklet. This is what you see under Section 1.

1. You want to know which forms to use. Where will you look for information?

2. You want to find out how to get help with your taxes. On which page will you find information?

3. You are filing a return in 1995. Is this the booklet you should be reading? Explain.

# Chapter Review

## Chapter Summary

- ☐ Tax laws and instructions can change quite often. English skills can help you cope with those changes.

- ☐ Begin by organizing your tax papers. Put them in categories, and then file them. For example, put all W-2s in one file folder and all 1099s in another filefolder.

- ☐ Tax instructions are found on the forms and in booklets. Read them slowly and carefully to understand them.

- ☐ Use a tax table to help you figure out the tax you owe.

- ☐ The tax booklet lists places for you to get help on your taxes. Libraries and tax preparation services can also help.

## Putting Skills Together

A friend tells you that you can file your tax forms late. But to do so, you must ask for an **extension**. How would you use the index of your tax booklet to find out how to file for an extension?

## Developing Writing Skills

Imagine that you've completed your income tax forms. You are getting $1200 back from the government! Write a short paragraph about how you will use the money.

## Chapter Quiz

Use a separate piece of paper to answer these questions. Write one or two sentences in each answer.

1. What are two skills that can help you file tax forms over the years?

2. What are two pieces of information that can be found on a W-2 form?

3. What tax information do you need from your bank?

4. Josh got the following pieces of information in the mail:

    Two W-2 forms; a 1099 on his savings account; a tax booklet; Forms 1040EZ and 1040; a 1099 on his checking account
    How could he organize them?

5. What is reading comprehension?

6. What are four steps to improve reading comprehension?

7. Suppose you want to know more about deductions. How would you go about looking up deductions in the tax booklet?

8. What is a tax table?

9. What piece of information do you need before you can use a tax table?

10. What three resources can you use to help you with your taxes?

## Vocabulary Review

Write three sentences of your own. Use the following vocabulary words at least once in each sentence:

income                    dependent                    itemize

# Unit Review

1. Which government office keeps birth certificates—city, county, or federal?

2. What proof of your age do you need to get a driver's license?

3. What must you do before you can vote for the first time?

4. Does a political candidate's campaign material show *bias*? Explain why or why not.

5. What is the quickest way to contact a government agency?

6. What is another name for a *measure* on a ballot?

7. How many amendments were passed to guarantee the vote to all Americans?

8. What is the deadline each year for filing your income tax?

9. What information is shown on a 1099 form?

10. What do the initials IRS stand for?

11. Name two places you can go to get help with your taxes.

12. If you double your income next year, will you have to pay more taxes?

# Unit Six

# English for Health and Safety

# Chapter *18* Getting Health Care

*Health care services are easier to find and use if you have good English skills. Most health services are listed in the telephone book.*

## Chapter Learning Objectives

☐ List health care services found in the telephone book.

☐ Write questions to ask during a health care visit.

☐ Use the library to learn more about health and health care.

☐ Interpret key information on medicine labels.

## Words to Know

**generic**   without a brand name

**pharmacist**   person who fills prescriptions

**physician**   medical doctor

**prescription**   a doctor's order for special medicine

**psychiatrist**   medical doctor who specializes in mental health treatment

**psychologist**   professional who specializes in mental health treatment

**specialists**   doctors who treat particular kinds of problems

**symptoms**   signs of illness

*Everyday English*
*Do you have the phone number of your doctor with you at all times? If not, where could you carry it?*

Jennifer lives on her own. She is one of those people who likes to say, "I've never been sick a day in my life."

One day, Jennifer wakes up with a sore throat. She has a headache and a fever. She stays in bed. But she seems to be getting worse, not better.

Jennifer does not have a doctor. But she decides she had better find one. She uses her English skills to help her find a good doctor.

## How to Find Health Care

There are two good ways to find health care. The best way is to ask friends, family, and co-workers for recommendations. You can ask what they like about their doctors or dentists. They can also tell you about costs and nearby services.

But there may be times when family and friends cannot help you. Perhaps you have a health problem you do not want to talk about. Or perhaps you are new in town and don't know anyone. In such cases, pull out the phone book and put your English skills to work.

## Practical English Skill 1: Use the Phone Book to Find Health Care

The phone book lists many kinds of health care professionals. The following chart explains some of the most common headings in the phone book:

**English Tip**

*Your phone book probably has an index to the yellow pages. Use it to help find the health care services you need.*

| If You Need | Look Under |
| --- | --- |
| ☐ Health care | "**Physicians**" in the yellow pages |
| ☐ Tooth care | "Dentists" in the yellow pages |
| ☐ Help coping with problems, thoughts, feelings, or behavior | "Mental Health Services," "**Psychiatrists**," or "**Psychologists**" in the yellow pages |
| ☐ Special problems, such as drinking too much | Area of treatment, such as "Alcoholism" |

☐ Need help
   paying for
   treatment

"City or County Health
Services" in The Government
Listings of the white pages

☐ Family planning
   and women's
   health care

"Clinics" or "Obstetrics and
Gynecology" under
"Physicians" in the
yellow pages

---

## Practice

Use the chart to answer the following questions.
Write your answers on a separate piece of paper.

1. Think back to Jennifer at the beginning of the
   chapter. What heading should she look under in
   the yellow pages to get treatment?

2. A woman thinks she is pregnant. Under which
   headings could she look in order to get a
   pregnancy test?

3. You need to get your teeth cleaned. How do you
   find a health care person to do the job?

4. A man has been feeling sad and lonely for a long
   time. He thinks he needs professional help. How
   could he find it in the phone book?

## Practical English Skill 2: Find Specialists

Sometimes you need a **specialist** who treats only
one kind of condition. Notice the last listing in the
chart. It says that for family planning, you can look
first under Physicians, then under Obstetrics and
Gynecology. In the yellow pages, often there is a
section that groups doctors by type of practice.

This special section might be headed "Physician and Surgeon Guide." You might find headings for specialties such as these:

☐ Family and General Practice
  Doctors who treat most kinds of common illnesses

☐ Dermatologist
  Doctors who specialize in skin care

☐ Pediatrics
  Doctors who specialize in treating infants and children

When you need special health care, scan these headings. You might find a doctor to suit your needs.

## Practice

Scan the clipping from the yellow pages on the next page to answer these questions.

1. You have aching joints. A friend says you might have arthritis. You look up "arthritis" in the yellow pages. What does it tell you to do?
2. Where could you go for acne treatment?
3. What kinds of things do plastic surgeons do?
4. Michelle Dern is your family doctor. Under which heading would you find her number?

**Brush Up
on the Basics**

*Do you remember how to scan reading material? If you need help, turn back to page 22 for review.*

**Use Your Skills**

Could you use a dictionary to find out what a podiatrist does?

## PHYSICIAN & SURGEON GUIDE

### ARTHRITIS

See Rheumatology

### DERMATOLOGY (Skin)

| | | |
|---|---|---|
| **Mark Bonner** | 3099 E. 13th | 555-0098 |
| Dora Chui | | |

| Skin—Cancer—Moles—Acne | |
|---|---|
| Located near Market & 5th | 555-3247 |
| 674 5th Street | 555-9876 |

| | | |
|---|---|---|
| Patrick Donnely | 9908 Potter | 555-0987 |

### FAMILY & GENERAL PRACTICE (CONT'D)

| | |
|---|---|
| Michelle Dern | |
| Day Call | 555-0433 |
| Night Call | 555-6632 |

### PLASTICS & RECONSTRUCTIVE SURGERY

**Nina Smith**

Certified by American Board of Plastic Surgeons

Neck and Face Lifts

Scar Revision

Dermabrasion

**Tips for Making Appointments**

When you make an appointment, be prepared. Here are some tips:

1. Give your name and **symptoms**. Make sure the person can treat your problem.

2. If the person cannot help you, ask for the name of someone who can.

3. Ask about charges and payment. If you have a health plan, make sure the person will accept it.

4. Have paper, a pencil, and a calendar handy. Write down the appointment date and time.

## Practical English Skill 3: Take Part in Your Own Health Care

The year is 1542. John Thomas goes to his doctor. John has been having terrible headaches. "Well, we'll just have to bleed you," says the doctor to John.

John lets the doctor cut his arm open. The blood flows. John never questions his doctor about this treatment. "After all," John thinks, "doctors know a lot more than I do."

These days, many doctors believe that patients get well more quickly if they take part in their own health care. Your English skills can help you do this. First, it is good to write a list of questions for your health care professional. Why should you write them down? Doctors are often busy and in a hurry.

And you may be nervous and forgetful during the office visit. A written list of questions will help you and the doctor. Here are some questions you might ask:

1. Are there any treatments other than the one you are recommending?
2. Does this medicine have any side effects I should know about?
3. What can I do to prevent getting sick again?

Secondly, you can read about health. Your library has many books on health care. There are "self-help" books on looking and feeling better. The encyclopedia can acquaint you with many diseases and their causes. The card catalog and reference room are important tools for health care.

## Practice

Use a separate piece of paper to write the answers to the following questions.

1. Your dermatologist wants to remove a mole. He says it looks "suspicious." What are three questions you would ask?
2. You have a bad knee. You want to read about possible causes and treatments before you see a doctor. Explain how you would use the library to help you.

## Practical English Skill 4: Read Medicine Labels Carefully

**Words for Health**
*Look for the word* **generic** *on medicine labels. Generic drugs do not have brand names and are usually less expensive than those with brand names.*

Remember Jennifer at the beginning of the chapter? She found a doctor in the yellow pages. The doctor checked her symptoms and said she had strep throat. Jennifer went to a pharmacy and picked up a **prescription** from the **pharmacist**. She then read the label carefully before taking the medicine.

All medicine labels contain important information. They tell you how much and how often to take a medicine. Other important information on the label is:

☐  The medicine's name

☐  The number of refills you can get

☐  How many pills are in the bottle

Here is an example of a prescription medicine label and how to read it:

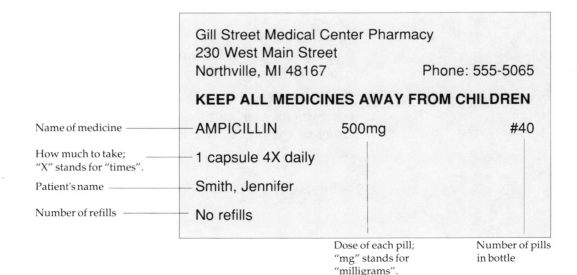

Gill Street Medical Center Pharmacy
230 West Main Street
Northville, MI 48167                    Phone: 555-5065

**KEEP ALL MEDICINES AWAY FROM CHILDREN**

Name of medicine —— AMPICILLIN          500mg                #40

How much to take; —— 1 capsule 4X daily
"X" stands for "times".

Patient's name —— Smith, Jennifer

Number of refills —— No refills

Dose of each pill;          Number of pills
"mg" stands for          in bottle
"milligrams".

## Practice

Answer the following questions using the prescription label on the facing page.

prescription label on the facing page.

1. What does the #40 mean?

2. How many refills can Jennifer get?

3. What does *mg* stand for?

4. How many pills should Jennifer take per day?

5. What is the name of the medicine Jennifer is taking?

6. Where did Jennifer have the prescription filled?

7. What warning is on the prescription label?

# Chapter Review

## Chapter Summary

☐ Find health care services by asking friends and family. Also use the telephone book.

☐ Look under different headings and scan telephone listings to find special services.

☐ Write down questions to ask your health care specialist.

☐ Use the library to learn more about health care and prevention of illness.

☐ Read key information on medicine labels for safety.

## Putting Skills Together

Choose one of the following health care topics. Write three questions you have about the topic. Then write two ways you could get those questions answered.

1. plague                  4. chicken pox

2. hair transplants        5. leeches and medicine

3. rhinoplasty             6. malaria

## Developing Writing Skills

Write about a health care experience. What made the experience good or bad? What would you have changed?

## Chapter Quiz

Use a separate piece of paper to answer the following question.
Write one or two sentences in each answer.

1. What are two ways to find health care services?

2. You want family planning advice. How do you use the phone book to help get it?

3. What section of the phone book can help you find specialists? Give an example.

4. What should you have by the phone when you are making an appointment?

5. Why should you write down questions before you see the doctor?

6. How can you use the library to improve your health care?

7. Why would you bother reading a medicine label?

8. You read this on a medicine label: 2 pills 3x after meals. What does it mean?

9. What does "mg" stand for on medicine labels?

10. What are two other pieces of information on medicine labels?

## Vocabulary Review

On a separate piece of paper, write three sentences of your own. Use at least one of the following words in each sentence:

specialists                pharmacist                generic

# Chapter *19* Living Safely

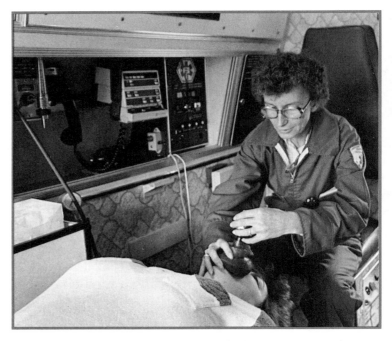

*Keeping an emergency aid by the telephone can save time and maybe even someone's life. English skills can help you prevent emergencies as well as respond to them.*

## Chapter Learning Objectives

☐ List emergency numbers found in the telephone book.

☐ Write one "emergency aid" for home use.

☐ Recognize ten "survival" words.

☐ Interpret safety information, warnings, and first aid instructions on labels.

## Words to Know

**antidotes**   remedies or treatments for poisoning

**crisis hotlines**   emergency numbers

**external**   outside

**hazard**   danger

**internal**   inside

**Emergency Tip**
*When you call a poison control center, have the medicine or poison container in front of you. The person who answers the phone may want you to read ingredients or other information listed on the label.*

Nick is baby-sitting two-year-old Pamela. While Nick is watching TV, Pamela toddles over. "See?" she says, and she hands him a bottle.

Nick takes a close look. It is an empty bottle of prescription medicine. Did Pamela take the medicine, or did she find the bottle empty? When Nick asks Pamela, she just giggles.

If you were Nick, would you know what to do?

### Call for Help

In emergencies, the key phrase is "Act fast, stay calm." And the two best friends you have are the telephone book and the telephone.

Most communities have a 911 emergency number. You can use this number for any life-threatening emergency. This can include fires, crimes, and accidental poisoning. If your community does not have a 911 number, look in the front of the white pages. You will find police and fire emergency numbers. You will also find **crisis hotline** numbers.

One example of a crisis hotline number is the poison control center. Anyone can call this number and get advice on poisons and their **antidotes**.

## Practical English Skill 1: Write an Emergency Aid

Even looking in the phone book can take time. So it is a good idea to make an emergency aid for your home. If you are a baby sitter, you can also make one on the job. An emergency aid might include phone numbers for

☐ Police department, fire department, and poison control center

☐ Helpful neighbors

☐ Children's doctor and medical insurance information

☐ Relatives to call in case of emergency

**Emergency English**
*Where is the best place to keep an emergency aid in your home?*

Keep the emergency aid by the main phone. You might cover it with plastic wrap to keep it clean. On the next page is one person's emergency aid, set up in chart form.

| In an emergency, call | Phone Number | Address |
|---|---|---|
| Police | 911 | |
| Fire Department | 911 | |
| Poison Control | 555-3348 | |
| Dr. Lubblow | 555-8760 | 777 Oscar Street, Oakland |
| Tom Parker (neighbor) | 555-8855 | 980 13th Street, Apt. 6 |
| Elsie June (neighbor) | 555-7120 | 975 13th Street |
| Nancy Lee (grandmother) | 555-9875 | 440 Green Street, Emeryville |

**Kids' HealthShield Medical Insurance Numbers:**

| | |
|---|---|
| Sara Ann Lee | 8903–90002BBD |
| Harry Lee | 7892–00934AAC |

## Practice

Write your own home emergency aid. Use the white pages to find emergency phone numbers. Include at least one family member or neighbor who should be called in case of emergency.

## Practical English Skill 2: Interpret Words That Mean Danger

You can keep many emergencies from ever happening. How? By reading and paying attention to the words around you.

Here are ten important words or phrases you should know. When you see one of them, take note. It could save your life or someone else's.

*Emergency English*
*What other kinds of emergency aids could you write for your home?*

| Ten Survival Words for Safety | |
|---|---|
| COMBUSTIBLE FLAMMABLE INFLAMMABLE | Nearby heat or fire could cause an explosion. |
| FOR EXTERNAL USE ONLY NOT FOR INTERNAL USE | For use only on the outside of the body. |
| NOXIOUS | Harmful to health in some way. |
| CONTAMINATED | Poisoned or pollutued |
| CONDEMNED | This sign is usually seen on buildings. It means they are unlivable or dangerous and must be torn down. |
| PROHIBITED | Stay away from or do not use. |
| DO NOT INHALE FUMES | Do not breathe near the product or site. |

## Practice

Use a separate piece of paper to answer these questions.

**Everyday English**
What other common warning signs do you see every day?

1. A spray can is labeled INFLAMMABLE. Where should you store it?

2. A building is labeled CONDEMNED. What does that mean?

3. A sign in front of a river says, CONTAMINATED. Should you swim in the river? Explain.

4. What does NOXIOUS mean?

5. A bottle is labeled "For **external** use only. Not for **internal** use." What would you do if a child drank from the bottle? Why?

## Practical English Skill 3: Read Safety Information

**Brush Up on the Basics**

How are your reading comprehension skills? If you need to practice them, turn to page 211 for advice.

In Chapter 17, you practiced your reading comprehension skills. Use these same skills when you read product labels and safety instructions. Remember to read one sentence at a time slowly. Then ask yourself, "What does that mean to me?" before you go on. Here are some common situations where you will need to read safety information:

☐ Before using household products and medicines Always read the labels.

## Skills for Safety

*Do you know much about first aid? Use your English skills to look up the nearest Red Cross chapter. The Red Cross offers first aid classes regularly. You can also get books on safety and first aid from your library.*

☐ When doing repairs

Read about safety **hazards** and procedures in manuals and on tools. If you are working near electricity, call a professional for help.

☐ If there is a child in the house

Get a book on home safety from the library. It will give you tips on covering up light sockets, locking cupboards, and more.

## Practice

Read the following label. Then use a separate piece of paper to answer the questions on the next page.

---

**BLEACH**

**IMPORTANT:**

DO NOT MIX WITH ANY HOUSEHOLD CLEANING AGENT EXCEPT SOAPS AND DETERGENTS. MIXING MAY PRODUCE NOXIOUS FUMES.

WARNING: Do not get on skin or eyes. If splashed on eyes or skin, flood with water for 15 minutes. Call a physician.

If taken internally, give milk or bread soaked in milk, followed by cooking oil. Call a physician immediately.

**Back to Nick
and Pamela**
*Look back at the story
on page 233. If you were
Nick, what would you do?
If there is any hint of
poisoning, he should call
911 or poison control. It
is better to be safe than
sorry.*

1. With what can you mix the bleach?

2. What are noxious fumes?

3. What should you do if the bleach gets in your eyes?

4. Should you wear rubber gloves when you use this bleach?

5. What should you do if a child drinks the bleach?

# Chapter Review

## Chapter Summary

- ☐ Emergency numbers can often be found in the front of the white pages.

- ☐ An emergency aid by the telephone can save valuable time. An aid should include names and numbers of agencies, neighbors, doctors, and relatives.

- ☐ Preventing emergencies means paying attention and reading carefully. Safety information can be found on household products, in manuals, and in books.

## Putting Skills Together

In Chapter 11, your wrote step-by-step job aids for work. You can write step-by step aids for emergencies in your home, too.

Read the article below. Then, on a separate piece of paper, write a numbered, step-by-step emergency aid for a family who lives in earthquake territory.

*Do you live in an earthquake zone? If so, you should have a home earthquake kit handy. This kit should include clean drinking water, a flashlight, and some dried foods. If a severe earthquake hits while you are home, get under a table or stand in a doorway. After the earthquake, leave the house as quickly as possible. If you smell gas, turn off any home gas lines. (Get your local utility company to show you how before an earthquake hits.) Fire caused by gas and electrical lines is actually one of the biggest hazards after an earthquake hits.*

## Developing Writing Skills

Write a paragraph about a common safety hazard in your life. Include three ways you can protect yourself from that hazard.

## Chapter Quiz

Use a separate piece of paper to answer the following questions. Write one or two sentences in each answer.

1. Where can you find emergency phone numbers?

2. Why is it a good idea to have an emergency aid by the phone?

3. What are three things that should be included on an emergency aid?

4. What should you have right in front of you when you call a poison control center. Why?

5. What does *Combustible* mean?

6. What does it mean if something is *Prohibited*?

7. Where might you see the phrase *For External Use Only*, and what does it mean?

8. Why should you read labels on household products before using them?

9. What should you do before you use a power saw for the first time?

10. How would you find a library book on home safety for children?

## Vocabulary Review

Match the words on the left to their meanings on the right. Write the numbers and corresponding letters on a separate piece of paper.

1. antidote                    a. outside

2. crisis hotlines             b. inside

3. internal                    c. emergency numbers

4. external                    d. treatment for poisoning

# Unit Review

1. Some people go to a hospital emergency room for ordinary medical care. Name two pros and cons about doing this.

2. Which doctor would you choose—a name you found in the phone book or a name recommended by a friend? Explain.

3. How can reading an encyclopedia help you stay healthy? Give an example.

4. Imagine that you are going to visit a doctor for the first time. Write a list of three questions you want to ask the doctor about your condition.

5. Suppose you have just picked up your prescription medicine from the drugstore. You don't understand the directions on the label. Who should you ask for help?

6. Where could you find doctors listed according to their specialties?

7. What medicine is most often used as an *antidote* for a headache?

8. Is cough syrup meant for *internal* or *external* use? How about shaving lotion?

9. How would you feel if there were a *noxious* condition in your home? Explain.

10. What kind of class could you take to help you prepare for medical emergencies?

11. Write a short paragraph about a time when you or someone you know stayed calm in an emergency.

12. Are things that are *prohibited* usually safe to do? Give an example.

# Unit Seven

# English for Recreation

**Chapter 20**

Reading Newspapers
and Magazines

**Chapter 21**

Traveling, Eating Out,
and Cooking

# Chapter 20 Reading Newspapers and Magazines

*Newspapers and magazines give you a lot of information for very little money. Using the index can help you quickly find the sections you want to read first.*

## Chapter Learning Objectives

☐ Use the index and headlines to find articles and features in newspapers.

☐ Identify the difference between hard news and soft news.

☐ Find key information in news articles.

☐ List three places to find magazines.

☐ Fill out a magazine subscription card.

## Words to Know

**current events**   things that are happening now

**headlines**   titles of newspaper articles

**subscribe**   to order

**subscription**   form for ordering a magazine

Cynthia and Wally sit in their living room with the TV on. It is a hot summer day. They are slumped on the couch.

"I'm bored," says Cynthia. "Let's do something."

"What do you want to do?" asks Wally.

"I don't know. What do you want to do?" asks Cynthia.

"I don't know."

If only Cynthia and Wally had good English skills! They could use newspapers and magazines to put some zip into their lives. Here's how.

### Read All About It

*Everyday English*
*What are the names of the local newspapers in your area? How much do they cost?*

You can use the newspaper for all kinds of things. Do you feel as if you're not interesting? Use the newspaper to keep up on the national and local news. Then form an opinion about what is happening. Are you ever as bored as Cynthia and Wally are?

Use the newspaper to find out about concerts, sports, and free events. Are you feeling sad and lonely? Read the comics or the advice column. Or challenge yourself with a daily crossword puzzle. All this and more is yours for fifty cents a day or less.

## Practical English Skill 1: Find What You Want

**Brush Up on the Basics**

*Do you remember how to scan headings? If you need help, turn to page 22 for review.*

How long would it take you to read every word in the newspaper? Probably hours and hours. Practically no one reads the entire newspaper. Most people read only what interests them. Way back in Chapter 2, you scanned the headings in books to find areas of interest. You can do the same with newspapers. Use **headlines** to help you find what you want. Headlines have key words that tell what an article is about.

## Practice

Use a separate piece of paper to answer these questions.

*Think English*
*Newspaper headlines come in different sizes. What do you think the different sizes mean?*

1. Read the headlines below. Then write a sentence or two explaining what you think you would find in that article.

   a.  **SPACE PROBE FINDS NO LIFE ON MARS**

   b.  **Top Singer to Perform Free in Park**

   c.  **PRESIDENT SPEAKS TO NATION ON AIR POLLUTION**

   d.  **Happenings About Town**

2. Of the four headlines, which article interests you the most? Why?

## Practical English Skill 2: Use the Newspaper Index

In addition to headlines, you can use a newspaper's index to help you find areas of interest. The index is usually placed at the bottom of the first page of the newspaper. Take a look at the following index.

**How Is It Different?**

*How is an index in a newspaper different from an index in a book?*

| INSIDE | | | |
|---|---|---|---|
| Autos | C17 | Horoscope | B2 |
| Books | E5 | Letters | A24 |
| Bridge | B7 | Movies | E4 |
| Business | C1 | Obituaries | B7 |
| Chess | B7 | People | B3 |
| Classified | B8 | Radio | E6 |
| Comics | B2 | Sports | D1 |
| Crossword | A25 | TV | E6 |
| Events | E1 | Theaters | E2 |
| Editorials | A24 | Weather | C18 |

Notice that types of articles and features are listed in alphabetical order. The letter and number following each listing tell you

☐ The section of the newspaper in which you will find the article or feature. The front section is always "A."

☐ The page number on which to look.

For example, suppose you want to look at the want ads in the Classified listings. The Classifieds are in section B on page 8.

## Practice

Use a separate piece of paper to answer these questions.

1. Where will you find the movie listings?
2. Suppose you are thinking about buying a new car. What section has articles that would interest you?
3. Does this newspaper have a crossword puzzle?
4. Where would you find your horoscope?
5. Where would you look to find out if your favorite baseball team won or lost last night?

## Practical English Skill 3: Read the News

You will find most of the "hard news" stories in the first section of the newspaper. Hard news stories are important **current events** happening in the world. A hard news story may be about a tornado or a war in the Middle East.

**English Skills**
*Can newspapers help you be a smart buyer? How?*

"Soft news" stories are meant to entertain or inform you. One soft news story told of a moose who had fallen in love with a cow. (It's true!) Other soft news stories focus on local plays, movies, people, and events.

One thing is true about both hard and soft news stories. The most important facts are in the first part of the article. Most news writers try to answer the who, what, where, when, and why questions in the first few paragraphs. That way, the reader can get the most important information quickly and easily. If the article interests you, you can read further.

## Practice

Read the news story. Then use a separate piece of paper to answer the questions.

---

### WAREHOUSE EXPLODES! THREE ESCAPE

April 17

A Richmond warehouse loaded with paint exploded at 11:15 last night. Three workers escaped without injury. The warehouse, located at 5th and Tennessee streets, caught on fire at approximately 10:30 p.m. Heat from the fire caused 5000 gallons of paints to explode and blast the roof off the building. Firefighters controlled the blaze by 2:00 this morning.

A night security officer and two workers escaped the burning building before the explosion. All are in good condition. No other injuries were reported.

Fire officials do not know the cause of the fire at this time.

"I'm glad I wasn't in there when it went," said security guard Rocky Brookens. "It was as if a bomb went off. I'm lucky to be alive."

---

1. What is the story about?
2. Where did the fire occur?
3. Who was involved?
4. When did it happen?
5. Why did it happen?
6. Is this a hard news story or soft news story? Why?

## Practical English Skill 4: Use Magazines

Magazines are a great resource for many things. Crafts magazines can help you learn how to knit, sew, build gliders, and more. There are magazines to keep you fit and help you get a job. News magazines cover current events in more detail than newspapers.

**Brush Up on the Basics**

*Do you remember how to use the* Reader's Guide to Periodical Literature? *Turn back to page 40 if you need to review.*

The best place to find a magazine that interests you is the library. You can browse through the magazine area or periodical room to find interesting magazines. Or you can use the *Reader's Guide to Periodical Literature* to find articles that interest you. Many stores and newsstands have magazine racks, too. And of course, your doctor's waiting room is well-stocked with magazines waiting to entertain you.

When you pick out a magazine, scan the table of contents. This important skill will help you find articles of the most interest to you.

### Practice

The following table of contents is from a news magazine. Look it over, and then answer the questions on a separate piece of paper.

WORLD EVENTS: Russian-U.S. Relations Today ........12
NATIONAL EVENTS: New Life for Old Cities ................36
HEALTH: New Hope for Bald Heads .............................51
EDUCATION: Computers in Schools ...........................62
SPORTS: Home Run King Strikes Out ..........................79
LAW: Death Row for Teenagers ...................................98
TRAVEL: The Ten Best Getaways ...............................109

1. Sid is planning a vacation in August. Can this magazine help him? If so, how?

2. Tom has noticed that his hairline isn't what it used to be. Is there anything in this magazine for him? If so, what?

3. Suzanne has to do a report for school on an international issue. What section in this magazine would give her some ideas?

## Practical English Skill 5: Subscribe to a Magazine

**English in Your Life**
*Is there a magazine that you especially like? What makes it enjoyable to you?*

Many times, a magazine will have only one or two articles of interest to you. But suppose you are a true sports fan. You want to read anything and everything about sports. You might want to **subscribe** to a sports magazine. If you subscribe, the magazine will come right to your home. Often, the cost per magazine drops when you subscribe, too.

The easiest way to subscribe is to buy a copy of the magazine. Inside you will usually find a **subscription** card. Look for this key information on the card:

☐ How much the subscription costs

☐ The time periods for which you can subscribe

☐ How to pay for the magazine

When you know what you want, fill in the card. Then enjoy your magazine!

## Practice

Below is a sample subscription card. Read it over, and then answer the following questions on a separate piece of paper.

---

### MEGAVIEW MAGAZINE

Last Name      First Name      Middle Initial

Street No.                 Apt. No.

City      State      Zip Code

DON'T PAY $2.00 AN ISSUE AT THE NEWSSTAND. SAVE MONEY AND HAVE MEGAVIEW DELIVERED RIGHT TO YOUR OWN HOME.

Check one:

____ I want 12 issues (one year) for $19.95

____ I want 24 issues (two years) for $37.95

____ I want 36 issues (three years) for $54.95

Check your method of payment:

____ Check or money order enclosed.

____ Bill me later.

1. For what time periods can you subscribe?

2. How much money do you save when you subscribe for one year?

3. You want to pay for the subscription now. Do you have this choice? Explain.

Now, suppose you have subscribed to MEGAVIEW Magazine. What makes this the perfect magazine for you? Use your imagination to answer the following questions.

4. What type of magazine is this?

5. Create a table of contents making up titles for articles you would like to read.

6. Who or what would have to be on the cover of this magazine for you to buy it at the store?

# Chapter Review

---

## Chapter Summary

☐ Newspapers and magazines are an inexpensive way to stay in touch with the world around you. You can use them to learn about current events and entertainment.

☐ Newspapers contain many features and articles. Some are soft news, and others are hard news. Use headlines and the index to find the articles of most interest to you.

☐ News articles answer the who, what, where, when, and why questions. Usually, the most important information is in the first few paragraphs.

☐ Magazines on many subjects can be found in the library and on newsstands. Use the table of contents to find articles of the most interest to you. Subscribing to a magazine can save you money and time.

## Putting Skills Together

In the next two days, take notes on an event that happens around you. It can be soft news or hard news. Then write a short article. Answer the who, what, where, when, and why questions in the first two paragraphs.

## Developing Writing Skills

Imagine a world without newspapers. What would change? How would information be passed along? Would businesses suffer? Would the world become a better or worse place? Write a short story about the "newspaperless" world. Give examples.

## Chapter Quiz

Use a separate piece of paper to answer the following questions. Write one or two sentences in each answer.

1. What are two reasons to read the newspaper?
2. What are two features in newspapers that could help you find entertainment?
3. Explain how headlines can save you time.
4. Name three types of articles or features that might be listed in the index.
5. An index lists the Comics on E-15. What does that mean?
6. Give two examples of a hard news story.
7. Give two examples of a soft news story.
8. How are hard news stories and soft news stories alike?
9. What are three places where you could look through magazines?
10. Why might you subscribe to a magazine?

## Vocabulary Review

Match the words on the left to their meanings on the right. Write the numbers and corresponding letters on a separate piece of paper.

1. headlines
2. current events
3. subscribe
4. subscription

a. form for ordering a magazine
b. titles of newspaper articles
c. to order
d. things that are happening now

# *21* Traveling, Eating Out, and Cooking

*Practical English skills have a place in recreation as well as at work. Whether you're reading a menu or planning a trip, you will need to understand what you read.*

## Chapter Learning Objectives

☐ Interpret words in context.

☐ Identify abbreviations and follow directions in recipes.

☐ List three resources to use for planning trips.

☐ Compare travel information.

## Words to Know

**à la carte**   separate

**agenda**   list of things to do

**brochures**   booklets

**entree**   main course

**ingredients**   what a prepared food contains

**recipe**   directions for preparing food a certain way

**reservations**   arrangements to save a place

**toll free**   without a charge

Robert is reading the food section of the newspaper. He comes across a restaurant review. This is what he reads:

"This restaurant is a great find. The food is rich and full of flavor. The entrees, especially the lemon swordfish, are wonderful."

Robert doesn't know what "entree" means. Does that mean he shouldn't try the restaurant? Of course not. He simply uses his English skills to figure out the meaning of the word.

## Practical English Skill 1: Figure Out What Words Mean

Since Robert is at home, he could look up "entree" in the dictionary. But suppose he is not at home. He could figure out the meaning of the word by

1. Studying how it is used in the sentence
2. Using his own experience
3. Making an "educated guess"

Here is an example:

**Just Ask**
*Some people are afraid to ask the meanings of words on a menu. Should they be?*

☐ Robert reads the sentence, "The entrees are wonderful, especially the lemon swordfish.

☐ He knows that lemon swordfish is a food, so he knows that the word **entree** has something to do with food.

☐ He's had fish at restaurants before, always for the main course. He decides that entrees are probably main courses.

This time, Robert is right. He may not always be right. But this skill of making educated guesses is very useful whenever you come across new words. This will happen a lot in restaurants and when you are traveling. Take a look at the menu on page 259. Then make your own "educated guesses" about what some of the words mean.

## WELCOME TO

# ZAP'S DINER

### Today's Menu

## Appetizers

green salad ...........................................2.95
ma's chicken soup ..............................1.95
fresh raw vegetables ..........................3.95

## Entrees

meat loaf..............................................7.95
fried chicken .......................................5.95
red snapper .........................................6.95
hamburger ...........................................4.95

(All entrees served with choice of potato and soup or salad, or à la carte for $1.00 less)

## Desserts

ma's apple pie ....................................2.95
ice cream .............................................2.45
cheese cake ........................................2.95

### Today's *prix fixe* meal:

fresh green salad, grilled fish, steamed vegetables, baked potato, and ma's apple pie

Only   $8.95

**Practice**

Use the menu to answer the following questions. Write your answers on a separate sheet of paper.

1. Look at the word "appetizers." Which of the following do you think has the same meaning:

   a. sweets    b. starters      c. main course

   Write one clue you got from the menu that helped you make your choice.

2. Find the sentence with the phrase "**à la carte**." Which of the following do you think has the same meaning:

   a. separately, without potato and soup or salad

   b. served on a cart

   c. baked instead of fried

   Write one clue in the sentence that helped you make your choice.

3. Find the words *prix fixe* (pronounced pree feeks) on the menu. Which of the following do you think has the same meaning:

   a. fresh fish

   b. fixed price

   c. free food

   Write one clue that helped you make your choice.

## Practical English Skill 2: Use a Cookbook

Suppose you have decided to have friends over to your home. For ideas about what to serve, you pull out a cookbook.

**Brush Up
on the Basics**

*Do you remember
how to use the table
of contents and the
index? Turn back to
pp. 18–20 if you need
to review.*

You can use many of the skills you have already practiced to find a good **recipe**. Suppose you're looking for a tasty salad. You look in the the table of contents and find a whole chapter on salads. Individual recipes or kinds of foods are also listed in the index. So if you know you want to make banana bread, just look in the index under *bananas* or *bread*. The chances are good that you will quickly find the page number that contains a recipe for banana bread.

Once you find a recipe, you will see a list of **ingredients**. Here is an example:

### Quick Banana Bread

1 lb mashed bananas

3/4 c sugar

1 egg

4 T butter, melted and cooled

1/2 c nuts, chopped

1 1/2 c flour

1 t salt

1 t baking soda

*Use Your Skills*

*What meal or type of
food would you like to
learn how to cook? How
could you go about
finding a recipe for it?*

The abbreviations lb, c, t, and T refer to amounts. Use the following chart to help you learn what they stand for.

| | | | | |
|---|---|---|---|---|
| lb: | pound | | c: | cup |
| oz: | ounce | | qt: | quart |
| tsp or t: | teaspoon | | min: | minute |
| tbl or T: | tablespoon | | | |

---

### Practice

On a separate piece of paper, write out the ingredients for quick banana bread. Do not use abbreviations.

---

## Practical English Skill 3: Follow the Directions

*A Quick Review*

*Where else in this book did you practice following directions?*

Recipes are simply directions. They tell you what to do. Read through the directions of a recipe twice before you begin. Make sure you are prepared. Then complete the steps one by one. If the recipe is good, your food will be good, too.

---

### Practice

Read the directions below. Then answer the following questions on a separate piece of paper.

#### Quick Banana Bread

Preheat oven to 325°. Lightly grease and flour a 9" X 5" loaf pan. Mash bananas in bowl. Beat in sugar, eggs, and butter. In another bowl mix flour, salt, and baking soda. Combine ingredients from both bowls. Pour into pan and bake 1 hour.

1. What size pan should you use?

2. How many bowls do you need?

3. What do you think "preheat" means?

4. About how much time will it take to make this bread, including preparation time?

## Practical English Skill 4: Plan a Trip

Suppose you want to plan a short trip. You can talk to people about places they've visited and liked. Or you can do some reading on your own.

There are many places to read about travel. Here are some of the best places to look:

- ☐ The travel section of the newspaper

- ☐ Guidebooks, found in libraries or bookstores

- ☐ **Brochures** from travel agents or auto clubs

- ☐ Travel magazines

*Use Your Skills*
*How could you use the phone book to find a travel agent?*

All of these resources can help you decide on the right trip. As you read, you will want to take notes and do some comparing. What are costs? What sights can you see? Is it a "city trip" or "country trip"? How will you travel?

These resources might also list ways you can get more information. Perhaps they will contain a **toll free** or 800 number. What should you do when you know where you want to go? Make **reservations**, or call a travel agent. Travel agents will make reservations and help you plan a trip at no cost to you.

## Practice

Use a separate piece of paper to write the answers to these questions.

1. How would you find guidebooks on Colorado in the library?

2. Read the following passages:

   Hot Springs Spa will take care of your every need. Free tennis lessons. The world's largest pool. Great food. The best of rooms. And those hot, soothing springs. Our low cost package is perfect for romantic couples: only $1,000 per week.

   Call Toll-Free 1-800-555-5555 today.

   Wilbur Park is a family campground. Swim in the gentle river. Let the kids enjoy the playground. Set up the tent and relax. Picnic tables and hot showers. $10.00 per night. Write Wilbur Park, P.O. Box 1009, Mill Valley, CA 94941.

   Write down the following information for each of these areas.

   a. types of activities

   b. who the vacation spot suits best

   c. cost

   d. how to get more information

3. Compare the vacation spots. Which suits your needs best? Why?

## Brush Up on the Basics

*Do you remember how to use the white pages and the yellow pages of the phone book? Turn back to page 194 if you need to review this skill.*

## More Tips for Travel

1. Write down your travel **agenda.** This is a day-by-day list of activities. It can also include travel information, phone numbers, and so on. It is a good way to organize your information.

2. Use your phone book skills to find tourist or visitor information offices.

3. Keep a notebook on your trip. Write down restaurants, things you see, and places you enjoy. You can share this information with friends or use it again someday.

4. Use map indexes and map keys to make traveling easier and more fun. Points of interest, such as parks, are on state maps as well as city maps.

| Date | Activities | Important Information |
|------|-----------|----------------------|
| Friday August 3rd | Fly to San Diego a.m. Spend day with Jim & Patty | Flight 3432, California Airlines |
| Saturday August 4th | See Balboa Park Dinner with Patrick | Visitors' Information 2688 Mission Bay Drive 555-8200<br><br>Patrick: 555-0988 |
| Sunday August 5th | Visit Old Town Lunch with Arlene and Sue Airport 4:15 p.m. | Arlene: 555-6321 Sue: 555-9840 Flight 1092 |

One person's travel agenda for a weekend in San Diego

# Chapter Review

## Chapter Summary

☐ Use the information surrounding unfamiliar words to make an "educated guess" about their meanings.

☐ Cookbooks are good tools. Use tables of contents and indexes to help you find recipes. Then follow the directions.

☐ There are many resources for planning a trip. Guides, brochures, and travel agents are the most important. As always, read for key information and take notes. Compare facts. Then find a trip to suit your needs.

## Putting Skills Together

Suppose you are taking a trip in your car. How could your English skills help you have a good trip? Give two examples.

## Developing Writing Skills

Describe the best trip you can imagine. Where would you go? What would you do? How would you get there? With whom would you go? Write at least eight sentences.

## Chapter Quiz

Use a separate piece of paper to answer these questions. Write one or two sentences in each answer.

1. Read this sentence:

   *Inside the cave are beautiful forms of helacite.*

   Take an educated guess at what "helacite" might be. Explain how you made that guess.

2. What are two ways to find out the meanings of words on a menu?

3. What are two ways to find a recipe for pot roast in a cookbook?

4. A recipe calls for 1 c flour. What does that mean?

5. A recipe calls for 2 lbs tomatos? What does *lbs* mean?

6. Where are three places to read about travel?

7. What are two kinds of things to compare when reading about different trips?

8. How can a travel agent help you take a trip?

9. Why is it a good idea to keep a notebook while you're on a trip?

## Vocabulary Review

On a separate piece of paper, write three sentences of your own. Use at least one of the following vocabulary words in each sentence:

à la carte                 agenda                 brochures

# Unit Review

1. Think about the last news report you saw on television or read in the newspaper. Name two *current events* that were discussed.

2. Imagine that there was a terrible train wreck in your town. Write a *headline* for a newspaper article about that accident.

3. Where does the index of a newspaper usually appear?

4. In what section of the newspaper will you find "hard news"?

5. What reference book in the library can help you find specific magazine articles?

6. In what section of the newspaper would you place an ad for a lost dog?

7. Which of the following is an entree—a slice of pie, a steak, or a bowl of soup?

8. 4 cups = 1 quart. Write out this measurement fact in a complete sentence.

9. Imagine that you are looking through a cookbook for a fudge recipe. You might find it in the index under *fudge*. Where else might you find it in the index?

10. How is a recipe like a tire repair manual?

11. Think about a dish that you know how to fix. What are two of its *ingredients*?

12. Why is it a good idea to make hotel *reservations* before you leave on a trip? What could happen if you didn't?

# English for Personal Expression

**Chapter 22**

Writing Personal Messages

**Chapter 23**

Using Criticism

*Personal letters and cards are important ways of staying in touch with other people. Practical English skills make letter-writing easy.*

## Chapter Learning Objectives

☐ List three "whens and whys" for sending cards.

☐ Use details to write personal messages in cards and letters.

☐ Write and answer invitations.

## Words to Know

**formal**   organized and following rules

**inexpensive**   not costing too much

**occasion**   special time or event

**RSVP**   French for "please respond"

**sympathy**   feelings of sorrow for someone else's loss

Jake is sitting at a table. In front of him is a small card and a piece of paper. He stares blankly into space for ten minutes. What's so hard? He is trying to write a thank-you note.

*Everyday English*
*Is it easier for you to write business messages or personal messages? Why?*

Writing personal cards and letters is hard for a lot of people. What should you say? How should you say it? Do you sometimes say nothing at all because you are afraid of saying the wrong thing?

There will be many times in your life when you will need to write a personal note to someone. Some of those times may be for happy reasons. Other times you may be writing for sad reasons.

Writing a personal note is an important skill to have. With some thought and time you can learn how to show your feelings with words.

This chapter will help you practice some writing skills for personal messages.

## Practical English Skill 1: Add Personal Messages to Cards

Sending cards is an easy thing to do. Cards are a nice way to show that you remember and care about someone. They can cheer people up and make them feel appreciated. Cards are an **inexpensive** way to send a message long distance. And they can come in handy for awkward **occasions**. For example, **sympathy** cards can be sent to the family of a person who died. Cards can also be used to "break the ice" when you want to let someone know you care.

Here are just a few examples of kinds of cards you can find in stores today:

| | | |
|---|---|---|
| birthday | wedding | anniversary |
| sympathy | graduation | get well |
| Christmas | Hanukkah | Mother's Day |
| Father's Day | congratulations | thank you |

You can, of course, just buy these cards, sign your name, and send them off. Why bother adding personal messages?

There are good reasons for doing so. Personal messages help you show special friendship, caring, and concern. In only a minute or two, you can add extra meaning to your cards.

### Practice

Do the following on a separate piece of paper.

1. Write two reasons that people don't bother to send cards at all.

2. Write two reasons that people should send cards at special times.

3. Write one reason to add personal messages to cards.

## Practical English Skill 2: Make It Personal

There is one key word to writing personal messages: details. Details could be called small items or little facts. They do not have to be important.

The details you include in a personal message should have a special meaning for the person to whom you are writing. Here is an example of a personal thank-you message:

Dear Andy,

The sweater you gave me is lovely. The color of blue is just perfect. Lots of people have told me I look great in it. Thank you for thinking of me on my birthday.

Sincerely,

Mary

Notice the details in the note. Mary mentions the gift (sweater), its color (blue), and how she looks in it (great). When Andy gets the card, he'll feel that Mary truly appreciates the sweater.

## Practice

Imagine that a friend has sent you three new pairs of socks. On a separate piece of paper, write the friend a personal thank-you message. Include at least three details to make the message personal.

## Practical English Skill 3: Write Personal Messages in Difficult Situations

Suppose you are writing a thank-you note for a gift that you really don't like. Or you are sending a sympathy card to a family. What should you say in these difficult situations?

**English in Your Life**
*If there were a death in your family, would you appreciate personal messages on cards?*

In difficult situations, you must consider the other person's feelings. Keep the notes short, but show your caring or appreciation. On a sympathy card, you might write something like this: "My thoughts are with you. Let me know if I can help." Or you can make it more personal by adding a happy memory. Here is an example:

"John was a good friend. He was always there when I needed him. I will miss him, too."

Thank-you notes for unwanted gifts should be kept simple. Just say, for example, "Thanks again for the feathered hat. I'll remember it always." Don't lie. And remember, it's the thought that counts!

## Practice

On a separate piece of paper, write a personal message for one of the following situations:

☐   Your friend's grandfather has just died

☐   Your aunt has given you a book you do not want to read

## Practical English Skill 4: How to Write Postcards

You're relaxing on the Hawaiian island of Maui. The beach is long and white. Every day your tan gets a little darker. You taste fresh, strange fruits at breakfast. At night, you dance under the stars with a new friend.

The time comes to write a postcard home. You quickly write, "Wish you were here," and sign your name. After all, what else is there to say?

Actually, there is a lot to say. Details about the trip can make the card more interesting for your family and friends. Here is an example:

> Dear Stanley,
>
> Hawaii is wonderful. The beaches are long and beautiful. I spend my days tasting tropical fruits and swimming. Tomorrow, I plan to try windsurfing. Oh, by the way, I might be in love. You'll hear more about that when I return. See you on the 16th.
>
> > See you soon,
> >
> > Mike

Before Mike wrote the postcard, he thought about interesting things he had done. He thought about what his friend Stanley would find interesting. He picked out a few details and put them on the card. His friend cannot wait to see Mike and ask him about his new girlfriend.

## Practice

In Chapter 21, you wrote a short description of your dream vacation. Now write a postcard home from that vacation. Include at least three details about the trip. (Make them up, of course!)

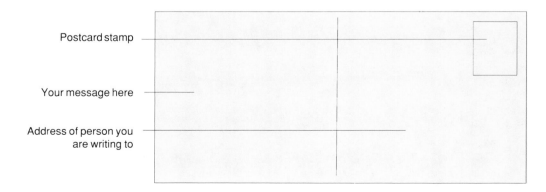

Postcard stamp

Your message here

Address of person you are writing to

## Practical English Skill 5: Write and Answer Invitations

Let's party! This is a phrase most people like to hear. Most of the time, news of a party is passed along by telephone. But for a more **formal** party, it's a good idea to send out written invitations. That way, you can plan food and drinks for the right number of people.

You can buy printed invitations at most card shops. They usually help you answer the who, what, when, where, and why questions. All you have to do is fill in the blanks. Here is an example:

BIRTHDAY PARTY!

FOR: _____

WHERE: _____

WHEN: _____

WHAT TO WEAR: _____

WHAT TIME? _____

RSVP: 555-3039 BY _____

**Regrets Only**

*Sometimes, invitations say "Regrets Only" and give a phone number. What do you think this means?*

Notice the letters **RSVP** at the bottom of the invitation. They stand for *respondez s'il vous plait*. That's French for "Please respond." Always call and let the host know whether you are coming or not. This is considered ordinary courtesy. Otherwise, you may not be invited to any more parties.

## Practice

Write an invitation to your next birthday party. Make up the details. Be sure to answer the who, what, when, where, and why questions.

## Practical English Skill 6: Write Personal Letters

It's easy to pick up the phone and call your family and friends long distance. But it's not always easy to pay the phone bill. Letters are an inexpensive way to communicate. Letters are also a good place to write about special feelings you have for someone.

Like personal messages on cards, letters should be full of details. If you've been too busy to write, explain why. If you have a new job, explain what you do. You have lots of room in a letter—use it.

Here is one example of a personal letter. Notice the details and the form.

> 3939 Dakota Street
> Worthington, OH 43085
> June 4, 1995

Dear Derek,

I'm sorry it's taken me so long to write. I've been really busy. For one thing, I just started a new job. I'm working as a grocery bagger at Green's. I work three hours each afternoon after school. It's a fast pace, so the time passes quickly.

What am I doing with all that money? I'm saving most of it for college. But some of it gets spent on Linda. Yes, we're still dating. Last week we drove to the mountains and went hiking.

Will you be back in July? Write and let me know the dates. It will be great to see you.

Sincerely,

*Stan*

**Use Your Skills**

*When is the next chance you'll have to write a card or letter? How can you make it personal?*

You can see that personal letters are less formal than business letters. Just put your own address and date in the upper right corner. Close it with "Sincerely," or "Love," and your name. And remember, if you are taking the trouble to send a card or letter, make it worthwhile. Put a little of yourself into it!

## Practice

Pretend that your best friend has moved away. Write the person a letter on a separate piece of paper. Explain what has been happening in your life. Include at least ten details. Use the same form as the letter on pages 278–279.

# Chapter Review

## Chapter Summary

☐ There are many occasions to send cards. You can make each card more meaningful by writing a personal message inside.

☐ Personal messages should be full of details. They can also focus on your feelings.

☐ For difficult situations, be honest. But be careful of hurting anyone's feelings.

☐ Invitations should include answers to the who, what, when, where, and why questions. RSVP means that you should let the host know if you are coming or not.

☐ Postcards are usually written by people who are traveling. They are more interesting when they include details of the trip and the person's activities.

☐ Letters are a chance to write many details. Personal letters are more informal than business letters.

## Putting Skills Together

Find an article or book about a place you have never been. Read a little about it. Take notes. Then imagine that you are writing a postcard home from that place. Include at least three details about what you are doing or seeing.

## Developing Writing Skills

Imagine that you have a "pen pal" in Europe. Write to the person. Include at least eight details about what life is like in America. Use the letter form found on pages 278–279.

## Chapter Quiz

Use a separate piece of paper to answer these questions. Write one or two sentences in each answer.

1. Name three occasions to send cards.
2. Explain why you would write a personal message inside a card.
3. What do good personal messages include?
4. Write an example of a personal thank-you message.
5. Write an example of a personal message for a sympathy card.
6. How can you save money by sending postcards?
7. At the bottom of an invitation are the letters RSVP. What does this mean, and why should you do it?
8. What should be included on every invitation?
9. What goes in the upper right corner of personal letters?
10. What are two ways to close personal letters?

## Vocabulary Review

Match the words on the left to their meanings on the right. Write the numbers and corresponding letters on a separate piece of paper.

1. RSVP          a. not costing too much
2. occasion      b. organized and following rules
3. formal        c. feelings of sorrow for someone else's loss
4. inexpensive   d. French for "please respond"
5. sympathy      e. special time or event

*Giving and receiving criticism is a part of life. Practical English skills help you use criticism to make your life better.*

## Chapter Learning Objectives

☐ Define criticism.

☐ List three uses for criticism in everyday life.

☐ Use four steps for giving effective criticism.

☐ List the best ways to respond to criticism.

## Words to Know

**compliments**    positive comments

**constructive**    useful

**criticism**    the act of making judgments

Dusty is dating Sharon. He likes a lot of things about her. For example, she is friendly and laughs a lot. But sometimes she makes fun of him in front of their friends. This makes him uncomfortable.

Dusty wants to say something to Sharon. But he is afraid she will become angry. Have you ever felt like Dusty? Is there a way for you to express feelings of anger or disappointment without causing a fight?

Yes, there are ways to explain why something or someone has upset you. At these times, it is important to pay attention to *how* you say something. So, even though you may be saying something negative, you will not cause an argument.

The English skills in this chapter can help. They focus on how you can use **criticism** to make your life better.

## Practical English Skill 1: Recognize Criticism

Perhaps you have seen movies reviewed on the TV. The reviewer outlines the good and bad things about a movie. You are hearing criticism of the movie.

Criticism is the act of judging a person or thing. People often think of criticism as only being bad or negative comments. "You'll never amount to anything, " is an example of a negative comment. But criticism can be positive comments, too. **Compliments** are a kind of criticism. You may look at someone and say, "That haircut is very flattering." You are judging the person's appearance. You are using criticism.

*Everyday English*

*Do you know someone who uses too much negative criticism?*

### Practice

Think of one time you received criticism. Was it positive or negative? How did it make you feel? Describe the experience on a separate piece of paper.

Now think of one time you gave criticism. Was it positive or negative? Did you consider the feelings of the other person? How did that person act? Describe the experience.

## Practical English Skill 2: Use Criticism in Your Everyday Life

You have personal relationships with many people such as your family, friends, and co-workers. And, of course, you have a personal relationship with yourself. You have to live with the things you do and with your feelings.

Criticism can improve your personal relationships. You can use it to express things you like and dislike. If you are clear in your criticism, you can make things change. You can help the good things to continue. You can get your feelings out in the open. And how about getting criticism? You can use self-criticism and criticism from others to improve yourself. Useful criticism is also called **constructive** criticism. People can use it to make their lives better.

### Practice

Use a separate piece of paper to answer these questions. Write one or two sentences for each one.

1. Give one example of negative criticism.
2. Give one example of positive criticism.
3. Which do you think is used more often? Why?

## Practical English Skill 3: Give Constructive Criticism

Sometimes, giving constructive criticism is easy. Sometimes, you may just want to give someone a compliment. Or you may know someone well enough that you feel comfortable saying anything. But many times, giving constructive criticism is difficult. Here are some steps you can use to make it easier.

### Step 1: Think Before You Speak

**Use Your Skills**
What works for you when you need to "think things over"?

Do you know someone who complains all the time, no matter what? Do you know someone who says things in anger or just to be mean? That person is not being constructive. The first step in giving constructive criticism is to think before you speak or act. Perhaps this means counting to 10 when you feel angry. Or maybe it means running around a track when you feel sad or upset. Getting control of your feelings is really a skill. Only you can find what works best for you.

### Step 2: Analyze the Situation

Take the time to *analyze* the situation. Look for both negative and positive points. In Dusty's case, he doesn't like it when Sharon teases him. It makes him uncomfortable in front of his friends. But there are positive things, too. He likes Sharon. He likes being around her. If he didn't, he wouldn't even bother trying to solve the problem.

**What Would Happen If?**
*Suppose people never bothered to use criticism? Would the world be a better place or a worse place?*

## Step 3: Decide What You Want

Finally, think about what you would like to see happen. Many times, people complain without a purpose. Nothing makes them happy. To give constructive criticism, you should have a goal in mind. In Dusty's case, he wants Sharon to stop teasing him. He hopes they can continue to see each other.

## Step 4: Put It Together

It's time for you to give your criticism. It is a good idea to start off with something positive. Then give the negative criticism. Try not to blame the other person. It is best to just state facts and feelings. Say what you want to have happen. Try to focus on solving the problem. If the other person gets emotional, stay calm. Here is how Dusty gave Sharon constructive criticism:

Dusty: *Sharon, I really like you. In fact, I like our relationship a lot. I want to keep seeing you. That's why I'm bringing this up. Sometimes, I feel uncomfortable when you tease me. Especially in front of our friends. What do you think we can do to solve the problem?*

Sharon: *So, you don't like me when we're with our friends? You think I am mean?*

Dusty: *I like you a lot. I just feel uncomfortable when you tease me. I'd feel better if we could talk about it.*

Notice that Dusty did not blame Sharon. He explained how he felt. He explained what was causing his feelings. And he focused on trying to solve the problem.

**Everyday English**
*What is the difference between complaining and giving constructive criticism?*

## Practice

Jill's parents just got divorced. Jill lives with her mother. Jill loves her mother. They've always been more like friends than mother and daughter. But lately, Jill's mother is yelling at her all the time. She says things like, "You dress like a slob. You spend too much time away from home. Why can't you help out more?" One day, Jill feels herself getting ready to lash back at her mother.

On a separate piece of paper, write what Jill should do or say. Use the four steps for giving constructive criticism.

## Using Criticism

Imagine that a friend says, "You're my friend. I care about you. I'm telling you this because I think you should know. You have bad breath."

What's the first thing that happens? Maybe you feel embarrassed. Maybe you're hurt. Being able to use criticism is a skill, too, just as giving it is.

When you are criticized, put your feelings aside for a moment. Otherwise, you may not be able to think clearly. Say to yourself, "Is this good information? Can I make myself better in some way by using it?"

What if the criticism is not constructive? Like Jill on this page, you can turn it around. Analyze the situation. Then use some constructive criticism of your own to solve the problem. Sometimes, a person will continue to be critical and complaining, no matter what. In such cases, ignore the criticism. But always take the time to think about it before you do.

### When You Criticize Yourself

Many times, people criticize themselves. And often, it is negative criticism. "I'm no good." "Why did I say that? It was stupid." "I'll never make it." This is negative criticism. And it is useless.

Turn your thoughts into constructive criticism. Try using these tips.

1. Pay attention to your thoughts. When you are being negative, stop. Then say something nice about yourself.

2. Give yourself constructive criticism. Don't just think about *what* you need to do better. Think about *how* you can do it better. Solve the problem.

3. When something bad happens, ask yourself, "How can I make this positive?"

4. Be willing to ask for help when you want to change. You will find that most people will admire you for asking.

**Use Your Skills**
*How can you use constructive criticism in the workplace?*

# Chapter Review

## Chapter Summary

- ☐ Criticism can be positive or negative. Constructive criticism contains a little of both.

- ☐ Constructive criticism can be used to improve your personal relationships.

- ☐ Constructive criticism involves thinking before acting. It means analyzing a situation for good and bad points. There should be a goal to constructive criticism.

- ☐ Try being open to criticism. Think about it, and turn it into something positive. Remember that you can use criticism to make your life better.

## Putting Skills Together

Find a review of a restaurant, movie, or other entertainment in the newspaper. Separate the comments into "positive" and "negative." Write them on a separate piece of paper.

## Developing Writing Skills

Think about a situation in which you could use constructive criticism. Write what you might say to cause a change. Look back at Dusty's words on page 287 for an example.

## Chapter Quiz

Use a separate piece of a paper to answer these questions. Write one or two sentences in each answer.

1. What is negative criticism? Give an example.
2. What is a compliment? Give an example.
3. What is constructive criticism?
4. How can you use constructive criticism to make your personal life better?
5. You want to think before you act. What are two ways to calm yourself down when you are upset?
6. You are having a problem. You decide to analyze the situation. What do you look for?
7. Imagine that your friend really bothers you at the movies. He's always shifting around in his seat. What might your goal be when giving him constructive criticism?
8. Suppose your friend becomes angry when you give him criticism. What should you do?
9. A friend tells you that you're too noisy at parties. What are two ways to handle the criticism?
10. A person goes to a party. He tells a joke that no one understands. He feels stupid. The next morning, he keeps seeing himself at the party. "I was really a jerk," he says to himself. How could this person turn his thoughts into constructive criticism?

## Vocabulary Review

Use each of the words below in a sentence. Write the sentences on a separate piece of paper.

compliment          criticism          constructive

# Unit Review

1. Why is it important to write a personal message in a birthday card? What does it show?

2. What would be an appropriate message to write on an anniversary card?

3. What kinds of details should be included in a thank you note? Give an example.

4. What can you say in a thank-you note to somebody who gave you a gift you didn't like?

5. Which are more formal—personal letters or business letters? Explain.

6. Suppose you receive an invitation to a party. You already have plans for that night. How do you respond to the invitation? Name two ways.

7. Think about a good friend of yours. Write a compliment about that person.

8. Think about someone you have trouble getting along with. Write one sentence of negative criticism about that person.

9. Think about your own good points and bad points. Give yourself a one-sentence compliment about one of your good points. Then write one sentence of constructive criticism about a change you need to make.

10. Recall the last movie you saw. Write a critical review of that movie. Mention both its strengths and weaknesses.

11. List the four steps you must take in order to give someone *constructive criticism*.

12. Name two ways you can criticize yourself constructively.

# Appendix

Glossary

Reference
Guide

Index

# Glossary

**à la carte**   separate

**accomplishments**   things done well

**acronym**   an abbreviation based on first letters of words in a title or slogan, as BART for Bay Area Rapid Transit

**action verbs**   words that show action, like cook and clean

**ad copy**   spoken or written words in advertising

**agenda**   list of things to do

**almanac**   book published each year that lists many facts, statistics, and other kinds of information

**analyze**   to figure something out; to interpret information

**annual fee**   yearly charge

**antidotes**   remedies or treatment for poisoning

**appendix**   additional information found in the back of a book

**application**   form employers ask job-seekers to fill out with information about themselves

**atlas**   book that contains maps of cities, states, countries, and continents

**back issues**   previous, non-current issues of magazines or newspapers

**balance**   amount

**ballot**   a list of people running for office; also a list of local laws that must be voted on

**benefits**   extras, such as health insurance, for workers

**bias**   an attitude that is strongly or unfairly on one side of an issue

**birth certificate**   official record containing a person's family and birth information

**body language**   messages given by the body

**brochures**   booklets

**call number**   the Dewey Decimal number by which a nonfiction book is arranged on a library shelf

**caption**   words that tell about an illustration

**card catalog**   file that contains list of books by title, subject, and author

**carpool**   group of people who share car rides

**check register**   record book for checks

**communication**   giving and receiving information

**comparative**   word used when saying how two things are alike or different

**compliments** positive comments

**confident** being sure of oneself

**cons** reasons against

**constructive** useful

**consumer** a person who buys goods and services

**cover letter** short letter to the employer included with job application or résumé

**co-workers** fellow workers

**credit reference** person or business who can vouch that a person pays his or her bills

**crisis hotlines** emergency numbers

**criticism** the act of making judgments

**current events** things that are happening now

**deductions** money taken from a paycheck for taxes and other things

**dependent** a person who is supported by another

**deposit** money that is put in an account; to put money in an account

**Dewey Decimal System** system of numbering library books

**duty** task performed on a job

**edit** to improve writing by making changes

**editorial** a statement of opinion

**election** choosing of government leaders or local laws by vote

**emotions** feelings

**entree** main course

**essay test** test that asks a person to write at least one paragraph on a certain subject

**estimate** guess at what something will cost

**evidence** proof; statements that say something is true

**extension** a longer period of time to file taxes

**external** outside

**fact** information that can be measured or proved as true

**fee** money charged for a service

**fiction** literature such as novels and short stories

**formal** organized and following rules

**generic** without a brand name

**glossary** at the back of a book, a list of definitions of special words in the book

**goals** things a person wants to achieve

**hazard** danger

**headlines** titles of newspaper articles

**illustration** drawing or photograph

**income tax**   money paid to the government, based on the amount of money made during the year

**index**   at the back of a book, a list of subjects and the page numbers on which they can be found

**inexpensive**   not costing too much

**ingredients**   what a prepared food contains

**interest**   percent earned or charged on money

**interests**   concerns or hobbies

**internal**   inside

**intersection**   the place where two streets cross each other

**itemize**   to list, as deductions

**job aid**   anything that helps a person do his or her job efficiently

**key words**   the most important written or spoken words in a sentence, paragraph, or text

**landlord**   person who owns rental property

**lease**   written contract between landlord and tenant

**literature**   writings in print

**main idea**   the central thought or idea of information that is written or spoken

**memo**   short note

**military**   having to do with the army, navy, or other defense group

**minimum**   least

**network**   the people you contact to help you get information about jobs

**nonfiction**   literature that is about true-to-life events or subjects

**not applicable**   does not apply

**objective test**   test that asks a person to choose one answer over another

**obligated**   having responsibility for something

**occasion**   special time or event

**opinion**   information based on a person's experience or thoughts; not a fact

**organizing**   putting things into clear order

**periodicals**   magazines

**personal reference**   person who can vouch for a person's good character

**personnel department**   a company department that hires employees and helps them solve problems

**pharmacist**   person who fills prescriptions

**physician**   medical doctor

**points of interest**   interesting things to do and see

**policies**   a company's rules

**prescription**   a doctor's order for special medicine

**presentation**   the act of showing or explaining something to another person or group

**procedure**   the steps in which a task is accomplished

**product**   something for sale that has been manufactured or grown

**promotion**   advancement to a job with more responsibility

**pronounce**   to say a word aloud

**proofread**   to carefully check writing for mistakes

**proposition**   a local or state law, or measure, that must be voted on

**pros**   reasons for

**psychiatrist**   medical doctor who specializes in mental health treatment

**psychologist**   professional who specializes in mental health treatment

**public transportation**   vehicles like buses and subways that are available for anyone to use

**recipe**   directions for preparing food a certain way

**reference section**   a section of the library containing the most-used books

**refundable deposit**   money that can be returned if certain conditions are met

**register**   to sign up

**reservations**   arrangements to save a place

**résumé**   written statement of a person's work experience, education, and personal information

**role model**   a person you want to be like and learn from

**route**   a certain path or direction

**RSVP**   French for "please respond"

**scan**   to quickly look through written material

**service**   a skill that a person offers, such as washing a car

**service contract**   a written agreement to provide a service

**short-answer test**   test that asks a person to write one or two sentences to answer a question

**slang**   informal language that is not considered part of standard English

**specialists**   doctors who treat particular kinds of problems

**Statement of Earnings and Deductions**   part of a paycheck stub telling how much money was earned and how much was deducted

**subscribe**   to order

**subscription**   form for ordering a magazine

**summarize**   to write or tell the major events or ideas without using details

**sympathy**   feelings of sorrow for someone else's loss

**symptoms**   signs of illness

**table of contents**   at the beginning of a book or magazine, a list of chapters or articles

**task**   small part of a large job

**tax deduction**   costs that can be subtracted from yearly income to help lower taxable income (such as health care costs)

**taxable income**   income that is taxed by the government

**tenant**   renter

**toll free**   without a charge

**topic sentence**   a sentence that introduces the subject or states the purpose

**transaction**   an exchange, usually involving money

**trend**   a general movement in a certain direction

**utilities**   gas, electricity, and water

**visualization**   imagining

**vouch**   to speak in favor of; to say that something is true

**warranty**   guarantee on a product or service

**withheld**   held back

# Reference Guide

## Sentences

---

### Grammar 1. Definition of a sentence

A sentence is a group of words that expresses a complete thought. Every sentence must have a subject and a predicate. (See Grammar 3-6) Every sentence begins with a capital letter and ends with a punctuation mark.

>That leopard has already killed 400 people.

>Is it still hungry?

>Be careful!

Sometimes a sentence may have only one word. (See Grammar 5.)

>Listen. Hurry!

---

### Grammar 2. Kinds of sentences

There are four different kinds of sentences.

A *declarative sentence* makes a statement. A declarative sentence ends with a period.

>A volcano in the Canary Islands is for sale.

An *interrogative sentence* asks a question. An interrogative sentence ends with a question mark.

>Who would want to buy a volcano?

An *imperative sentence* gives a command. An imperative sentence ends with a period.

> Show me the list of buyers.

An *exclamatory sentence* expresses excitement. An exclamatory sentence ends with an exclamation point.

> They must be crazy!

## Grammar 3. Subjects and predicates in declarative sentences

Every sentence has two main parts, the subject and the predicate. The subject names what the sentence is about. The predicate tells something about the subject.

In most declarative sentences, the subject is the first part. The predicate is the second part.

> A famous sea captain      was often sick.
>
> He      suffered from seasickness.

In some declarative sentences, the predicate is the first part. The subject is the second part.

> Back and forth rolled  the captain's ship.

## Grammar 4. Subjects and predicates in interrogative sentences

Every interrogative sentence has a subject and a predicate. In some interrogative sentences, the subject is the first part. The predicate is the second part.

> Who      solved the mystery?
>
> Which clue      was most important?

In most interrogative sentences, part of the predicate comes before the subject. To find the subject and predicate, rearrange the words of the interrogative sentence. Use those words to make a declarative sentence. (The declarative sentence will not always sound natural, but it will help you.) The subject and predicate of the two sentences are the same.

| Why did | the butler | lie about it? |
|---|---|---|
| The butler | did lie about it why? | |

## Grammar 5. Subjects and predicates in imperative sentences

Only the predicate of an imperative sentence is spoken or written. The subject of the sentence is understood. That subject is always you.

(You)   Try an underhand serve.

(You)   Please show me how to do it.

## Grammar 6. Subjects and predicates in exclamatory sentences

Every exclamatory sentence has a subject and a predicate. In most exclamatory sentences, the subject is the first part. The predicate is the second part.

Kotzebue Sound, Alaska,    is frozen over nearly all of the time!

In some exclamatory sentences, part of the predicate comes before the subject.

What terrible weather that city    has!

(That city    has terrible weather!)

## Grammar 7. Compound subjects in sentences

A sentence with a compound subject has two or more subjects with the same predicate.

> **Jesse James and his brother Frank** were famous outlaws in the Old West.

> **Cole Younger, James Younger, and Robert Younger** were all members of the James gang.

## Grammar 8. Compound predicates in sentences

A sentence with a compound predicate has two or more predicates with the same subject.

> The postal workers **took in the tailless cat and named him Kojak**.

> Kojak **lives in the post office, catches mice, and earns a salary**.

## Grammar 9. Compound sentences

A compound sentence is made up of two shorter sentences joined by a coordinating conjunction. (See Grammar 45.) A compound sentence has a subject and a predicate followed by another subject and another predicate.

> G. David Howard set a record in 1978, and it remains unbroken.

> Howard told jokes for more than 13 hours, but not all of them were funny.

## Nouns

---

### Grammar 10. Definition of a noun

A noun is a word that names a person, a place, or a thing.

> That brave **man** crossed the **ocean** in a **rowboat**.

---

### Grammar 11. Singular and plural forms of nouns

Almost every noun has two forms. The singular form names one person, place, or thing.

> Only one **worker** in that **factory** can name the secret **ingredient**.

The plural form names more than one person, place, or thing.

> Several **workers** in those two **factories** can name the secret **ingredients**.

---

### Grammar 12. Spelling plural forms of nouns

For most nouns, add s to the singular form to make the plural form.

> joke—jokes    character—characters
>
> cartoon—cartoons

If the singular form ends in **s**, **ss**, **sh**, **ch**, or **x**, add **es**.

> bus—buses    witch—witches
>
> kiss—kisses    fox—foxes
>
> wish—wishes

If the singular form ends in a consonant and **y**, change the **y** to **i** and add **es**.

spy—spies    discovery—discoveries

mystery—mysteries

If the singular form ends in **f**, usually change the **f** to **v** and add **es**. If the singular form ends in **fe**, usually change the **f** to **v** and add **s**. There are some important exceptions to these rules. Look in a dictionary if you are not sure of the correct plural form.

half—halves    wife—wives

loaf—loaves    knife—knives

Some exceptions

roof—roofs    chief—chiefs    safe—safes

If the singular form ends in **o**, add **s** to some words and **es** to others. Look in a dictionary if you are not sure of the correct plural form.

studio—studios    tomato—tomatoes

piano—pianos    zero—zeros

Some nouns change in other ways to make the plural form.

child—children    mouse—mice

woman—women    goose—geese

A few nouns have the same singular form and plural form.

sheep—sheep    deer—deer

moose—moose

### Grammar 13. Proper nouns and common nouns

A proper noun is the special name of a particular person, place, or thing. Each word in a proper noun begins with a capital letter.

> Then **Max** stopped in **Junctionville** and ate a **Big Mac**.

A common noun is the name of any person, place, or thing.

> Then the **man** stopped in a small **town** and ate a **hamburger**.

### Grammar 14. Possessive nouns

The possessive form of a noun shows ownership. Usually the possessive form of a noun is made by adding an apostrophe and s. (See Punctuation 20.)

> A **piranha's** teeth are as sharp as razors.

The possessive form of a plural noun that ends in s is made by adding only an apostrophe. (See Punctuation 20.)

> Nobody believed the **explorers'** story.

### Grammar 15. Nouns of address

A noun of address names the person being spoken to. One or two commas separate a noun of address from the rest of a sentence. (See Punctuation 9.)

> Where are you going, **Ricky?**

> I told you, **Lucy,** that I have a rehearsal tonight.

## Grammar 16. Appositive nouns

An appositive noun renames or identifies the noun that comes before it in a sentence. An appositive noun is usually part of a group of words. The whole group of words is called an appositive. One or two commas separate an appositive from the rest of a sentence. (See Punctuation 10.)

A Ford was the preferred car of John Dillinger, **the famous gangster.**

Even his sister, **the president of her own company,** would not hire him.

## Verbs

## Grammar 17. Definition of a verb

A verb is a word that expresses action or being.

The volcano **erupted** suddenly.

It **was** a terrific surprise.

Almost all verbs have different forms to show differences in time.

Sometimes puffs of smoke **rise** from the volcano.

A huge cloud of heavy gray smoke **rose** from it last week.

## Grammar 18. Action verbs

Most verbs are action verbs. An action verb expresses physical action or mental action.

> The committee members **banned** Donald Duck comic books.

> They **disliked** the duck's behavior.

## Grammar 19. Linking Verbs

Some verbs are linking verbs. A linking verb tells what the sentence subject is or is like. The most common linking verb is be. (See Grammar 23.)

> A black and white dog **became** a mail carrier in California.

> The dog's name **was** Dorsey.

## Grammar 20. Verb phrases

A verb phrase is made up of two or more verbs that function together in a sentence. The final verb in a verb phrase is the main verb.

> The 13,000-pound bell **had disappeared**.

> Somebody **must have stolen** it.

The verbs before the main verb in a verb phrase are helping verbs. The most common helping verbs are forms of be (is, are, am, was, were), forms of have (has, have, had), and forms of do (does, do, did). (See Grammar 23.)

> That radio station **is sponsoring** a contest.

> The station **has** already **received** 45,217 postcards.

## Grammar 21. Agreement of verbs with nouns

Verbs that express continuing action or existence and verbs that express current action or existence are in the present tense. Almost all present-tense verbs have two different forms. These two different forms go with different sentence subjects. The verb in a sentence, or the first helping verb in a sentence, must agree with the most important word in the subject of that sentence.

One present-tense form of a verb agrees with singular nouns. This verb form ends with s.

> A tick **sucks** blood from larger animals.

The other present-tense form of a verb agrees with plural nouns.

> Ticks **suck** blood from larger animals.

## Grammar 22. Agreement of verbs with compound subjects

The present-tense verb form that agrees with plural nouns also agrees with compound subjects. (See Grammar 7.)

> Beth Obermeyer and her daughter Kristen **hold** a record for long-distance tap dancing.

## Grammar 23. Forms of the verb be

The verb be has more forms than other verbs. Be has three present-tense forms: is, are, and am. Is agrees with singular nouns. Are agrees with plural nouns. Am agrees with the pronoun I.

> Mary Lou Retton **is** a famous gymnast.

> Many people **are** her fans.

> I **am** a pretty good gymnast, too.

Most verbs have one past-tense form that tells about action or existence in the past. Be has two past-tense forms: was and were. Was agrees with singular noun subjects. Were agrees with plural noun subjects.

> The argument **was** noisy.

> Several neighbors **were** very angry about it.

## Grammar 24. Irregular verbs

Usually the past-tense form of a verb ends in d or ed.

> William Baxter **invented** an important part of the Morse code.

Some verbs change in other ways to form the past tense. These are called irregular verbs. Look in a dictionary if you are not sure of the correct past-tense form of a verb.

> Samuel Morse **took** all the credit.

## Pronouns

---

### Grammar 25. Personal pronouns

A personal pronoun is a word that takes the place of one or more nouns.

> Superman tried to enlist in the Army during World War II, but **he** was found unfit to serve.

---

### Grammar 26. Subject forms and object forms of personal pronouns

Each personal pronoun has a subject form and an object form. These different forms are used in different ways in sentences. (The pronouns it and you are the same in the subject form and the object form.) These are the subject forms of personal pronouns: **I, you, he, she, it, we, they.** These are the object forms of personal pronouns: **me, you, him, her, it, us, them.**

> **He** saw through a wall and read the wrong eye chart.

> The army did not accept **him**.

---

### Grammar 27. Antecedents of pronouns

A personal pronoun refers to the noun it replaces. That noun is the antecedent of the pronoun.

> **Roy Rogers** became famous in movies. **He** was usually accompanied by his horse, Trigger, and his dog, Bullet.

If a personal pronoun takes the place of two or more nouns, those nouns together are the antecedent of the pronoun.

> **Roy Rogers and Dale Evans** often worked together.
> **They** made dozens of movies.

---

## Grammar 28. Subject-verb agreement with personal pronouns

The present-tense verb form that agrees with singular nouns also agrees with the pronoun subjects **he, she,** and **it.**

> She **tests** new planes.

The present-tense verb form that agrees with plural nouns also agrees with the pronoun subjects **I, you, we,** and **they.**

> **They** test new planes.

---

## Grammar 29. Indefinite pronouns

A word that refers to a general group but does not have a specific antecedent is an indefinite pronoun.

> **Nobody** can be right about **everything.**

One common indefinite pronoun, **no one,** is written as two words.

## Grammar 30. Subject-verb agreement with indefinite pronouns

The present-tense verb form that agrees with singular nouns also agrees with most indefinite pronouns.

Almost everyone **remembers** the Alamo.

No one **knows** exactly what happened there.

Of the accounts written of the battle, several **claim** to be factual.

## Grammar 31. Possessive pronouns

A personal pronoun that shows ownership is a possessive pronoun.

These possessive pronouns are used before nouns in sentences: **my, your, his, her, its, our, their.**

Why are **my** gym shoes in **your** locker?

These possessive pronouns stand alone in sentences: **mine, yours, his, hers, its, ours, theirs.**

Are these gym shoes **mine,** or are they **yours?**

Unlike possessive nouns, possessive pronouns are not written with apostrophes.

## Grammar 32. Reflexive pronouns

A pronoun that refers back to a noun or pronoun in the same sentence is a reflexive pronoun. These words are reflexive pronouns: **myself, yourself, himself, herself, itself, ourselves, yourselves, themselves.**

> The witness had been talking to **himself.**

> You should have bought **yourself** a ticket.

## Grammar 33. Demonstrative pronouns

A word that points out one or more people or things is a demonstrative pronoun. These four words can be demonstrative pronouns: **this, that, these,** and **those.**

> **These** are the funniest cartoons.

> Nobody laughed at **those.**

If the word **this, that, these,** or **those** is followed by a noun, the word is not a demonstrative pronoun. (See Grammar 34.)

# Adjectives

## Grammar 34. Definition of an adjective

A word that adds to the meaning of a noun or pronoun is an adjective. Adjectives usually tell what kind, which one, or how many.

> **Those exhausted** men have been playing tennis for **nine** hours.

Adjectives that tell what kind can sometimes stand alone.

> They were **exhausted.**

Adjectives that tell which one or how many always come before nouns.

> **Both** players have used **several** rackets.

## Grammar 35. The adjectives a and an

The adjectives **a** and **an** are usually called *indefinite articles.* (The adjective **the** is usually called a *definite article.*) **A** is used before words that begin with consonants or with a "yew" sound.

> **A** penguin cannot fly.

> Cooking is **a** useful activity.

**An** is used before words that begin with vowels or with an unsounded **h**.

> **An** ostrich cannot fly.

> Brutus is **an** honorable man.

## Grammar 36. Predicate adjectives

An adjective that comes after a linking verb and adds to the meaning of the subject noun or pronoun is a predicate adjective.

> Maria Spelterina must have been **brave.**

> Her tightrope walks across the Niagara Falls were **dangerous.**

## Grammar 37. Proper adjectives

An adjective that is formed from a proper noun is a proper adjective. Each word in a proper adjective begins with a capital letter.

> The **American** dollar is worth less than the British pound.

> The new **Spielberg** film is great!

## Grammar 38. Comparative and superlative forms of adjectives

Adjectives can be used to compare two or more people or things. When only two people or things are compared, use the comparative form of an adjective. To make the comparative form, add **er** to adjectives with one syllable. Use **more** (or **less**) before some adjectives with two syllables. Look in a dictionary if you are not sure of the correct comparative form of an adjective.

> Buster Keaton was **funnier** than Charlie Chaplin.

> Buster Keaton was **more amusing** than Charlie Chaplin.

When more than two people or things are compared, use the superlative form of an adjective. To make the superlative form, add **est** to adjectives with one syllable and many adjectives with two syllables. Use **most** (or **least**) before some adjectives with two syllables and all adjectives with more than two syllables. Look in a dictionary if you are not sure of the correct superlative form of an adjective.

> Buster Keaton was the **funniest** movie actor who ever lived.

> Buster Keaton was the **most amusing** movie actor who ever lived.

The comparative and superlative forms of the adjective **good** are **better** and **best.**

> Buster Keaton was a **better** actor than Charlie Chaplin.

> Buster Keaton was the **best** movie actor who ever lived.

The comparative and superlative forms of the adjective **bad** are **worse** and **worst.**

> The Revenge of the Killer Tomatoes was a **worse** movie than The Fly.

> The Revenge of the Killer Tomatoes was probably the **worst** movie ever made.

## Adverbs

### Grammar 39. Definition of an adverb

A word that adds to the meaning of a verb or verb phrase is an adverb. Adverbs usually tell where, when, how, or how often.

> The rodeo rider **bravely** mounted the mustang **again.**

## Grammar 40. Comparative and superlative forms of adverbs

Adverbs can be used to compare the actions of two or more people or things. When only two people or things are compared, use the comparative form of an adverb. To make the comparative form, usually use **more** (or **less**) before the adverb. Add **er** to a few short adverbs.

Polly speaks **more clearly** than that other parrot.

Polly can fly **higher** than that other parrot.

When more than two people or things are compared, use the superlative form, usually use **most** (or **least**) before the adverb. Add **est** to a few short adverbs.

Of all those parrots, Polly speaks **most clearly.**

Of all those parrots, Polly can fly **highest.**

The comparative and superlative forms of the adverb **well** are **better** and **best.**

That parrot behaved **better** than your pet cat.

Of all the unusual pets in the show, the parrot behaved **best.**

The comparative and superlative forms of the adverb **badly** are **worse** and **worst.**

Your pet monkey behaved **worse** than that parrot.

Of all the unusual pets in the show, your cat behaved **worst.**

## Grammar 41. Using adjectives and adverbs

Use an adjective to add to the meaning of a noun or a pronoun.

> The **proud** actor accepted the prize.

Use an adverb to add to the meaning of a verb or a verb phrase. *Many (but not all) adverbs end in ly.*

> The actor accepted the prize **proudly.**

## Grammar 42. The adverb *not*

The adverb **not** changes the meaning of the verb or verb phrase in a sentence.

> The soldiers in the fort would **not** surrender.

> Help did **not** arrive in time.

## Grammar 43. Avoiding double negatives

The adverb **not** is a negative word. Other common negative words are **no, never, no one, nobody, nothing, nowhere, hardly, barely,** and **scarcely.** Use only one negative word to make a sentence mean **no** or **not.**

> **No one** ever understands how I feel.

> My friends **never** understand how I feel.

> **Hardly** anyone understands how I feel.

## Grammar 44. Adverbs used as intensifiers

Certain adverbs add to the meaning of adjectives or other adverbs. These special adverbs are sometimes called intensifiers.

> One **terribly** nosy neighbor heard the whole conversation.

> **Very** nervously, she told the police all about it.

# Conjunctions

## Grammar 45. Coordinating conjunctions

A word used to join two equal parts of a sentence is a coordinating conjunction. The most common coordinating conjunctions are **and**, **but**, and **or**.

> Many people have driven across the country, **but** these two men did it the hard way.

> Charles Creighton **and** James Hargis drove across the country **and** back again.

> They never stopped the engine **or** took the car out of reverse gear.

## Grammar 46. Subordinating conjunctions and complex sentences

A word used to begin an adverb clause is a subordinating conjunction. The most common subordinating conjunctions are listed below.

| | | | |
|---|---|---|---|
| after | before | though | when |
| although | if | unless | whenever |
| because | since | until | while |

An adverb clause is a group of words that has a subject and a predicate but that cannot stand alone as a sentence. An adverb clause functions like an adverb. It tells when, where, how, or why. An adverb clause usually comes at the end or at the beginning of a sentence. (See Punctuation 8.) A sentence formed from an adverb clause (which cannot stand alone) and a main clause (which can stand alone) is called a *complex sentence.*

Otto E Funk played his violin **while he walked from New York City to San Francisco.**

**When he finished his musical journey**, both his feet and his hands were tired.

**Whenever it is threatened**, an opossum plays dead.

It can be poked, picked up, and even rolled over **while it remains completely rigid.**

## Interjections

---

### Grammar 47. Definition of an interjection

A word that simply expresses emotion is an interjection. A comma or an exclamation point separates an interjection from the rest of a sentence. (See Punctuation 11.)

**Oh,** now it makes sense.

**Wow!** That's terrific news!

## Prepositions

---

### Grammar 48. Definition of a preposition

A word that shows the relationship of a noun or pronoun to some other word in a sentence is a preposition. The most common prepositions are listed below.

| | | | |
|---|---|---|---|
| about | before | during | over |
| above | behind | for | since |
| across | below | from | through |
| after | beneath | in | to |
| against | beside | into | under |
| along | between | like | until |
| among | beyond | of | up |
| around | by | off | upon |
| at | down | on | with |

## Grammar 49. Prepositional phrases

A preposition must be followed by a noun or a pronoun. The preposition and the noun or pronoun that follows it form a prepositional phrase.

> A new record **for sit-ups** was set **by Dr. David G. Jones**.

> His family and friends were very proud **of him**.

Often, other words come between the preposition and the noun or pronoun. Those words are also part of the prepositional phrase.

> He set a new record **for consecutive straight legged sit-ups**.

## Grammar 50. Objects of prepositions

A preposition must be followed by a noun or a pronoun. That noun or pronoun is the object of the preposition.

> One of the main **characters** of <u>Star Trek</u> didn't appear until the second **season**.

## Grammar 51. Personal pronouns in prepositional phrases

A personal pronoun that is the object of a preposition should be in the object form. These are object-form pronouns: **me, you, him, her, it, us, them**.

> The other presents for **her** are still on the table.

> The most interesting present is from **me**.

## Grammar 52. Prepositional phrases used as adjectives

Some prepositional phrases are used as adjectives. They add to the meaning of a noun or pronoun in a sentence.

> The Caribbean island **of Martinique** is a department **of the French government**.

## Grammar 53. Prepositional phrases used as adverbs.

Some prepositional phrases are used as adverbs. They add to the meaning of the verb or verb phrase in a sentence.

> **In 1763**, Napoleon Bonaparte's wife, Josephine, was born **on Martinique**.

# Sentence Parts

## Grammar 54. Simple subjects

The most important noun or pronoun in the subject of a sentence is the simple subject of that sentence. The object of a preposition cannot be the simple subject of a sentence.

> A 27-year-old **man** from Oklahoma swam the entire length of the Mississippi River.

> **He** spent a total of 742 hours in the river.

## Grammar 55. Simple predicates

The verb or verb phrase of a sentence is the simple predicate of that sentence.

> Actor W. C. Fields **may have had** 700 separate savings accounts.

> Fields **used** a different name for each account.

## Grammar 56. Direct objects

A word that tells who or what receives the action of a verb is the direct object of the verb. A direct object must be a noun or a pronoun. A personal pronoun that is a direct object should be in the object form. These are object-form pronouns: **me, you, him, her, it, us, them.**

> The first aspirin tablets contained **heroin.**

> A German company sold **them** for 12 years.

## Grammar 57. Indirect objects

A word that tells to whom (or what) or for whom (or what) something is done is the indirect object of the verb expressing the action. An indirect object comes before a direct object and is not part of a prepositional phrase. An indirect object must be a noun or pronoun. A personal pronoun that is a direct object should be in the object form. These are object-form pronouns: **me, you, him, her, it, us, them.**

> Professor Sommers gave his **students** the same lecture every year.

> He told **them** a familiar story.

## Grammar 58. Predicate nominatives

A word that follows a linking verb and renames the sentence subject is the predicate nominative of a sentence. A predicate nominative must be a noun or a pronoun. A personal pronoun that is a predicate nominative should be in the subject form. These are subject-form pronouns: **I, you, he, she, it, we, they.**

> The best candidate was **Andrea**.

> In my opinion, the winner should have been **she**.

# Capitalization Rules

## Capitalization 1. First word in a sentence

Begin the first word in every sentence with a capital letter.

> **Who** won the eating contest?

> **That** man ate 17 bananas in two minutes.

## Capitalization 2. Personal pronoun I

Write the pronoun **I** with a capital letter.

> At the last possible minute, **I** changed my mind.

## Capitalization 3. Names and initials of people

Almost always, begin each part of a person's name with a capital letter.

Toby Ohara                    Rosie Delancy

Sue Ellen Macmillan

Some names have more than one capital letter. Other names have parts that are not capitalized. Check the correct way to write each person's name. (Look in a reference book, or ask the person.)

Tim O'Hara                    Tony de la Cruz

Jeannie McIntyre

Use a capital letter to write an initial that is part of a person's name.

B. J. Gallardo                J. Kelly Hunt

John F. Kennedy

## Capitalization 4. Titles of people

Begin the title before a person's name with a capital letter.

**Mr**. Sam Yee              **Captain** Cook

**Dr**. Watson               **Governor** Maxine Stewart

Do not use a capital letter if this kind of word is not used before a person's name.

Did you call the **doctor**?

Who will be our state's next **governor**?

## Capitalization 5. Names of relatives

A word like grandma or uncle may be used as a person's name or as part of a person's name. Begin this kind of word with a capital letter.

> Only **Dad** and **Aunt Ellie** understand it.

Usually, if a possessive pronoun comes before a word like grandma or uncle, do not begin that word with a capital letter.

> Only **my dad** and **my aunt** understand it.

## Capitalization 6. Names of days

Begin the name of a day with a capital letter.

> Most people don't have to work on **Saturday** or **Sunday**.

## Capitalization 7. Names of months

Begin the name of a month with a capital letter.

> At the equator, the hottest months are **March** and **September**.

## Capitalization 8. Names of holidays

Begin each important word in the name of a holiday with a capital letter. Words like **the** and **of** do not begin with capital letters.

> They usually have a picnic on the **Fourth of July** and a fancy dinner party on **Thanksgiving**.

## Capitalization 9. Names of streets and highways

Begin each word in the name of a street or highway with a capital letter.

> Why is **Lombard Street** known as the most crooked road in the world?

## Capitalization 10. Names of cities and towns

Begin each word in the name of a city or town with a capital letter.

> In 1957, the Dodgers moved from **Brooklyn** to **Los Angeles**.

## Capitalization 11. Names of states, countries, and continents

Begin each word in the name of a state, country, or continent with a capital letter.

> The story was set in **Nevada**, but they shot the film in **Mexico**.

> There are very high mountain peaks in **Antarctica**.

## Capitalization 12. Names of mountains and bodies of water

Begin each word in the name of a mountain, river, lake, or ocean with a capital letter.

> Amelia Earhart's plane was lost somewhere over the **Pacific Ocean**.

## Capitalization 13. Abbreviations

If the word would begin with a capital letter, begin the abbreviation with a capital letter.

> On the scrap of paper, the victim had written, "**Wed.—Dr.** Lau."

## Capitalization 14. Titles of works

Use a capital letter to begin the first word, the last word, and every main word in the title of a work. The words **the**, **a**, and **an** do not begin with capital letters except at the beginning of a title. Coordinating conjunctions and prepositions also do not begin with capital letters. (See Grammar 45 and Grammar 48.)

> Archie and Edith were the main characters in the television series **All in the Family**.

## Capitalization 15. Other proper nouns

Begin each major word in a proper noun with a capital letter. A proper noun is the special name of a particular person, place, or thing. (See Grammar 13.) Usually, the words **the**, **a**, and **an**, coordinating conjunctions, and prepositions do not begin with capital letters. (See Grammar 45 and Grammar 48.)

> Jerry rushed to the **Burger King** and ordered three **Whoppers**.

## Capitalization 16. Proper adjectives

Begin each word in a proper adjective with a capital letter. A proper adjective is an adjective that is formed from a proper noun. (See Grammar 37.)

That **American** author writes about **English** detectives.

She loves **Alfred Hitchcock** movies.

## Capitalization 17. Direct quotations

Begin the first word in a direct quotation with a capital letter. (See Punctuation 14-16.)

Dr. Pavlik said, "**There** are simply no teeth in the denture law."

If the words that tell who is speaking come in the middle of a quoted sentence, do not begin the second part of a quotation with a capital letter.

"**There** are simply no teeth," said Dr. Pavlik, "**in** the denture law."

## Capitalization 18. Greetings and closings in letters

Begin the first or only word in the greeting of a letter in a capital letter.

**Dear** Mr. Lincoln:     **Dear** Uncle Abe,

Begin the first or only word in the closing of a letter with a capital letter.

**Sincerely** yours,     **Very** truly yours,

**Love,**

## Capitalization 19. Outlines

In an outline, begin the first word of each heading with a capital letter.

    II.  **Houses** by mail order

        A.  **First** sold by Sears, Roebuck in 1903

            1.  **Build**-it-yourself kits

            2.  **Included** all materials and instructions

        B.  **Other** companies now in business

In an outline, use capital Roman numerals to label main ideas. Use capital letters to label supporting ideas. For ideas under supporting ideas, use Arabic numerals. For details, use small letters. Use a period after each Roman numeral, capital letter, Arabic numeral, or small letter.

    I.  Miner George Warren

        A.  Risked his share of Copper Queen mine in bet

            1.  Bet on race against George Atkins

                a.  Warren on foot

                b.  Atkins on horseback

            2.  Lost property worth $20 million

## Punctuation Rules

### Punctuation 1. Periods, question marks, and exclamation points at the ends of sentences

Use a period, a question mark, or an exclamation point at the end of every sentence. Do not use more than one of these marks at the end of a sentence. For example, do not use both a question mark and an exclamation point, or do not use two exclamation points.

Use a period at the end of a declarative sentence (a sentence that makes a statement).

> A hockey player must be able to skate backward at top speed.

Also use a period at the end of an imperative sentence (a sentence that gives a command).

> Keep your eye on the puck.

Use a question mark at the end of an interrogative sentence (a sentence that asks a question).

> Who is the goalie for their team?

Use an exclamation point at the end of an exclamatory sentence (a sentence that expresses excitement).

> That was a terrific block!

## Punctuation 2. Periods with abbreviations

Use a period at the end of each part of an abbreviation.

Most titles used before people's names are abbreviations. These abbreviations may be used in formal writing. (**Miss** is not an abbreviation and does not end with a period.)

**Dr.** Blackwell               **Mr.** Bill Tilden

**Ms.** Maureen Connolly

Most other abbreviations may be used in addresses, notes, and informal writing. They should not be used in formal writing.

Lake View **Blvd.**            **Mon.** and **Thurs.**

Fifth **Ave.**                  **Dec.** 24

Do not use periods in the abbreviations of names of government agencies, labor unions, and certain other organizations.

Tomorrow night **CBS** will broadcast a special program about the **FBI**.

Do not use periods after two-letter state abbreviations in addresses. This special kind of abbreviation has two capital letters and no period. Use these abbreviations only in addresses.

Their new address is 1887 West Third Street, Los Angeles, **CA** 90048.

## Punctuation 3. Periods after initials

Use a period after an initial that is part of a person's name.

Chester **A.** Arthur          **C.C.** Pyle

Susan **B.** Anthony

## Punctuation 4. Commas in dates

Use a comma between the number of the day and the number of the year in a date.

Hank Aaron hit his record-breaking home run on **April 8, 1974.**

If the date does not come at the end of a sentence, use another comma after the number of the year.

**April 8, 1974,** was an exciting day for Hank Aaron's fans.

Do not use a comma in a date that has only the name of a month and the number of a year.

Aaron hit his final home run in **July 1976.**

Do not use a comma in a date that has only the name of a month and the number of a day.

**April 8** is the anniversary of Aaron's record-breaking home run.

## Punctuation 5. Commas in place names

Use a comma between the name of a city or town and the name of a state or country.

> The world's largest chocolate factory is in **Hershey, Pennsylvania.**

If the two names do not come at the end of a sentence, use another comma after the name of the state or country.

> **Hershey, Pennsylvania,** is the home of the world's largest chocolate factory.

## Punctuation 6. Commas in compound sentences

Use a comma before the conjunction—**and, but,** or **or**—in a compound sentence. (See Grammar 9 and Grammar 45.)

> Eighteen people tried, **but** no one succeeded.

## Punctuation 7. Commas in series

Three or more words or groups of words used the same way in a sentence form a series. Use commas to separate the words or word groups in a series.

> **Jamie, Mitch, Kim, Lou, and Pablo** entered the contest.

> Each contestant **swam one mile, bicycled two miles, and ran five miles.**

## Punctuation 8. Commas after introductory phrases and clauses

Use a comma after a phrase that comes before the subject of a sentence. A phrase is a group of words that usually functions as an adjective or an adverb. One kind of phrase is a prepositional phrase. (See Grammar 49.)

**In the old dresser,** Penny found the diamonds.

If the entire predicate comes before the subject of the sentence, do not use a comma. (See Grammar 3.)

In the old dresser lay the diamonds.

Use a comma after an adverb clause at the beginning of a sentence. (See Grammar 46.)

**When he was first named hockey's most valuable player,** Wayne Gretzky was only 18 years old.

## Punctuation 9. Commas with nouns of address

Use a comma after a noun of address at the beginning of a sentence. (See Grammar 15.)

**Fernando,** that was a teriffic pitch!

Use a comma before a noun of address at the end of a sentence.

That was a teriffic pitch, **Fernando!**

If the noun of address comes in the middle of a sentence, use one comma before the noun and another comma after it.

That, **Fernando,** was a teriffic pitch!

## Punctuation 10. Commas with appositives

Use a comma before an appositive at the end of a sentence. (See Grammar 16.)

> This costume was worn by George Reeves, **Hollywood's first Superman.**

If an appositive comes in the middle of a sentence, use one comma before the appositive and another comma after it.

> George Reeves, **Hollywood's first Superman,** wore this costume.

## Punctuation 11. Commas or exclamation points with interjections

Usually, use a comma after an interjection. (See Grammar 47.)

> **Well,** we should probably think about it.

Use an exclamation point after an interjection that expresses excitement.

> **Wow!** That's a terrific idea!

## Punctuation 12. Commas after greetings in friendly letters

Use a comma after the greeting in a friendly letter.

> **Dear John,**    **Dear Uncle Theodore,**

## Punctuation 13. Commas after closings in friendly letters and business letters

Use a comma after the closing in a letter.

**Love,**          **Yours sincerely,**

## Punctuation 14. Quotation marks with direct quotations

A direct quotation tells the exact words a person said. Use quotation marks at the beginning and at the end of each part of a direct quotation.

**"Look!"** cried Tina. **"That cat is smiling!"**

**"Of course,"** said Tom. **"It's a Cheshire cat."**

## Punctuation 15. Commas with direct quotations

Usually, use a comma to separate the words of a direct quotation from the words that tell who is speaking. (See Punctuation 16.)

Jay asked, "Who won the game last night?"

"The Cubs won it," said Linda, "in 14 innings."

## Punctuation 16. End punctuation with direct quotations

At the end of a direct quotation, use a period, a comma, a question mark, or an exclamation point before the closing quotation marks.

If the direct quotation makes a statement or gives a command at the end of a sentence, use a period.

> Linda said, **"The Cubs won last night's game."**

> Jay said, **"Tell us about the game."**

If the direct quotation makes a statement or gives a command before the end of a sentence, use a comma.

> **"The Cubs won last night's game,"** said Linda.

> **"Tell us about the game,"** Jay said.

If the direct quotation asks a question, use a question mark.

> **"Was it an exciting game?"** asked Jay.

If the direct quotation expresses excitement, use an exclamation point.

> Linda yelled, **"It was great!"**

## Punctuation 17. Quotation marks with titles of works

Use quotation marks around the title of a story, poem, song, essay, or chapter.

> **"Happy Birthday to You"** is the most popular song in the world.

If a period or a comma comes after the title, put the period or comma inside the closing quotation mark.

> The most popular song in the world is **"Happy Birthday to You."**

## Punctuation 18. Underlines with titles of works

Underline the title of a book, play, magazine, movie, television series, or newspaper.

> One of the best movies about baseball was <u>**The Natural.**</u>

## Punctuation 19. Apostrophes in contractions

Use an apostrophe in place of the missing letter or letters in a contraction.

> is not—**isn't**    Mel is—**Mel's**    I will—**I'll**

## Punctuation 20. Apostrophes in possessive nouns

Use an apostrophe and **s** to write the possessive form of a singular noun. (See Grammar 14.)

> This cage belongs to one bird. It is the **bird's** cage.

> This cage belongs to Tweeter. It is **Tweeter's** cage.

Use only an apostrophe to write the possessive form of a plural noun that ends in **s**.

> This is a club for boys. It is a **boys'** club.

Use an apostrophe and **s** to write the possessive form of a plural noun that does not end in s.

> This is a club for men. It is a **men's** club.

---

## Punctuation 21. Colons after greetings in business letters

Use a colon after the greeting in a business letter.

> **Dear Mrs. Huan:     Dear Sir or Madam:**
>
> **Dear Senator Rayburn:**

---

## Punctuation 22. Colons in expressions of time

When you use numerals to write time, use a colon between the hour and the minutes.

> **5:45** P.M.     **9:00** A.M.     **12:17** P.M.

---

## Punctuation 23. Hyphens in numbers and fractions

Use a hyphen in a compound number from twenty-one to ninety-nine.

> **thirty-seven     fifty-eight     seventy-three**

Use a hyphen in a fraction.

> **one-quarter     two-thirds     seven-eighths**

# Index